Praise for *Dance Like Nobody's Watching*

"Authenticity is a spiritual practice—and this book is a call to devotion. If you're ready to stop editing yourself and return to your internal power, this is your book. Michelle Wadleigh is an unapologetic wisdom teacher. In this book, she offers you the tools to unlock more self-awareness and true freedom to express. Get ready to dance!"

—Tama Kieves, bestselling author of *Learning to Trust Yourself* and *A Year Without Fear*

"*Dance Like Nobody's Watching* is a playful, soul-deep invitation to shed your armor, trust your wild inner wisdom, and fall deliciously in love with the most authentic version of yourself."

—Barbara Carrellas, author of *Urban Tantra* and *The Book of Ecstasy*

"*Dance Like Nobody's Watching* reads like a soul dream brought into waking life. With the grace of a seasoned spiritual guide, Michelle Wadleigh invites readers to awaken from limiting inner narratives and step into the life their soul has been dreaming them toward all along. Tender, empowering, and deeply affirming, it reminds us that self-love is not something we earn, but something we remember."

—Dr. Kelly Sullivan Walden, bestselling author of *Dreamifesting*

DANCE LIKE NOBODY'S WATCHING

ALSO BY MICHELLE WADLEIGH

Forgiveness: A Workbook for Emotional and Spiritual Freedom

Shadow Work: A Spiritual Path to Healing and Integration

Prosperous Me: Accepting the Bounty of My Birthright!

40 Days to Freedom: A Lenten Practice for the Modern Mind

DANCE LIKE NOBODY'S WATCHING

THE SOUL'S JOURNEY TO COURAGE, AUTHENTICITY, AND SELF-LOVE

MICHELLE WADLEIGH

ST. MARTIN'S ESSENTIALS
NEW YORK

First published in the United States by St. Martin's Essentials,
an imprint of St. Martin's Publishing Group

EU Representative: Macmillan Publishers Ireland Ltd, 1st Floor, The Liffey Trust Centre,
117–126 Sheriff Street Upper, Dublin 1, D01 YC43

www.stmartins.com

Designed by Steven Seighman

Library of Congress Cataloging-in-Publication Data is available upon request.

ISBN 978-1-250-42073-2 (trade paperback)
ISBN 978-1-250-42074-9 (ebook)

First Edition: 2026

10 9 8 7 6 5 4 3 2 1

This book is dedicated to all the women in my life—those I know intimately and those I hope to know more deeply.
To my mother, my grandmother, and all my aunts.
To my sisters: MaryJane, Myrtle, Maureen, and Margaret.
To my nieces and grandnieces, and to my granddaughters: Lila and Annaliese.
To my daughters-in-love: Isis and Julia.
To my chosen family and soul-friends: Gesa, Jo, Judi, Marcy, Marilynn, and to all my students and coaching clients who have entrusted me with their stories, their growth, and their hearts.
Here's to the strength of being a woman—to all we hold, all we lift, all we endure, and all we create.
Here's to the beauty and the burden of giving and sustaining life.
Here's to our brilliance, our resilience, our ancient knowing.
We are powerhouses.
We are mystical badass women.
And I celebrate each and every one of you.

CONTENTS

Foreword by Rev. Dr. David Alexander xi
MINDSHIFT: *Speaking the Language of Your Heart* xiii

INTRODUCTION 1
The Face of Spiritual Authenticity 7
The Shadows of Inauthenticity 13
The Inner Texture of Inauthenticity 16
Roots Before Wings—The Tools Laid Out . . . 25
Let's Go Home 31
1. *Reclaiming the Language of the Inner Voice* 33
2. *See Yourself with Brave and Honest Eyes* 51
3. *Asking the Questions That Wake You Up* 71
4. *Dismantling the Inner Judge* 90
5. *Standing in the Sacred Now of Your Being* 104
6. *Walking the Path of Forgiveness, the Path to Freedom* 118
7. *Learning to Turn Your Compassion Inward* 135
8. *Laying Down the Armor and Embracing All of You* 148
9. *Walking in the Unshakable Knowing of Who You Are* 162
10. *Remember, You Were Never Broken* 177
11. *Unleashing the Full Expression of Your Soul* 193
12. *Love Yourself Like Your Life Depends on It* 206

Appendix: Guidelines for a Silent Retreat 219

Resources 233

Mindshift: Speaking the Language of Your Heart 237

Mindshifts for Your Heart and Soul 243

Acknowledgments 249

About the Author 251

FOREWORD

Every once in a while there arises a voice so tuned to the heart of Spirit and the pulse of the human journey that it seems to sing a song we've always known but have forgotten how to hum. My friend Michelle Wadleigh is such a voice. Her newest offering, *Dance Like Nobody's Watching: The Soul's Journey to Courage, Authenticity, and Self-Love* is not merely a book—it is a transformational invitation to come home to yourself.

I have had the privilege of working alongside Michelle in ministry for many years. She is one of the colleagues I trust most—not only for her wisdom and teaching, but for her uncompromising commitment to truth-telling. Michelle is the rare kind of leader who will always speak the truth in love, always encourage from a place of fierce compassion, and always model the very authenticity she calls us into. What you will read here is not theory; it is a lived practice. It is the outpouring of a woman who has done her own work, faced her own shadows, and chosen—again and again—to stand in the light of her authentic self.

This book is at once deeply personal and universally accessible. Michelle does not shy away from the tender territory of inauthenticity—those moments when we wear masks, seek approval, or live by default rather than design. With courageous honesty, she even shares how these dynamics have shown up in her own life, whether in the midst of caregiving through her husband's illness, navigating long years in ministry, or simply choosing whether or not to clean the kitchen after a Super Bowl party. By offering her own stories, she gives us permission to find ourselves in the mirror of her words, and to tell the truth about our own.

What I love most about this work is the way it illuminates the path home. Each of the twelve paths Michelle offers is a spiritual practice in itself: reclaiming the power of self-talk, practicing radical honesty, giving ourselves permission to hide when needed, and learning to live from essence rather than performance. Through journal prompts, affirmations, and her powerful "spiritual mindshifts," she equips the reader with tools that are practical, grounded, and lovingly disruptive to the habits that keep us small.

What I know is that Michelle never confuses authenticity with self-indulgence. She reminds us that our authentic life is not only a gift to ourselves, but a gift to the whole of humanity. To stand unapologetically in our truth, to love ourselves without condition, to live without the weight of masks or pretense—this is how we bless the planet. As she writes, "There is no private good." Our freedom always ripples outward.

This is not just a book you read, it is a book you dance with, you cry with, you rise with. If you are brave enough to let it, it will help you remember that at your core there is a place that has never been harmed, a wellspring of pure authenticity that has been waiting for you all along.

So, take a breath. Step to the center of your own life. And, as Michelle so beautifully invites us, dance like nobody's watching—because the truth is, all of creation is watching, cheering you on, and longing for you to remember who you really are.

—Rev. Dr. David Alexander,
author of *Freedom from Discord: The Promise of New Thought Liberation Theology*

RevDAlexander.substack.com
revdavidalexander.com

MINDSHIFT

Speaking the Language of Your Heart

At the threshold of this new book, I encourage you to get in the middle of the dance floor as together we flow and sway and step our way into raising our standards for your life—right now.

I have a silly personal share for you. When I was quite young, I loved music but I never learned how to dance; and when my friends would take me out, I was the one who would stand on the edge of the dance floor tapping my feet. I was willing not to embarrass myself by being awkward in such a public way. Then one night, a friend said, "Just feel the rhythm; let the rhythm move you," and after a bit more of liquid encouragement, I did. I felt the rhythm, I let go, and I was never the same again. To this day, I love to dance, although I no longer care who might be watching and how anyone might be judging me.

There is a reality in which you no longer have to pretend to be what you are not, care about things you don't care about, be nice when you're actually angry and disgusted by someone's behavior. There is a reality in which you shed the layers of who you have learned to be so you can grab hold of the original you that was born to be fully expressed. And there is a reality in which you cease apologizing for who you are, never again have to defend your opinions or expend effort to get approval from the outside, and live up to your undiluted perfection. This reality is you being bold yet humble, strong yet sensitive, successful yet generous, confident and compassionate as one who walks through life choosing love as your response but not because of any outside pressure. This is the you that has been waiting to be.

This reality is your unspoken birthright. In this reality, you dress as you wish, prosper from your passion, speak from your heart, and think for yourself. This is the reality in which you live your life like an open book for all the world to read.

Now imagine yourself alone, immersed in and surrounded by breathtaking beauty. As you relax and absorb the quiet beauty of the world you are immersed in, an unexpected impulse arises within you—to close your eyes and journey inward. Not in a self-absorbed manner, but with a deep, profound curiosity about your inner landscape and the essence of what makes you uniquely you.

As this journey begins, imagine there is a path through a tunnel. While it might be dark, you know intuitively it is safe. Each step you take is met with just enough light to take your next step, so you never have to walk in the dark for long, because you are bringing the light with you. Your courage to continue forward and deeper turns to faith with every step. The deeper you venture, the more cocooned you feel, always curious and always safe. This feeling is similar to being in the womb of your ideal mother—safe and loving.

With every step forward, a new aspect of yourself is unveiled—a memory, a story, a feeling, a shadow. You walk slowly, and everything you see commands your attention. With a sense of awe, you begin to understand the construction of your SELF. As you go deeper, this inner path leads you to your authentic self, stripped of opinions, judgments, and self-criticism because you find greater understanding of why you became who you are.

> Imagine yourself free from the layers of identity you've picked up along the way, both self-imposed and shaped by society. Imagine yourself free.
>
> Imagine yourself strong enough to weather the journey. Imagine yourself steady enough to meet what arises.
>
> Imagine yourself worthy of your own unfolding, worthy of the truths you are about to uncover.

This is the sacred return—the journey from the human-constructed self to the authentic self you were ordained to be. Not to be someone new, but to remember the "you" you were born to be. Please accept this invitation with an open heart and mind. The rewards of this journey will appear before you right where you stand. I am not assuming that you need to be different, I am suggesting that you need to be YOU, as you begin to remember who you are.

HERE IS A QUICK EXAMPLE OF THE AUTHENTIC POWER PRACTICES OFFERED THROUGHOUT THE BOOK.

Take a comfortable seat or gently rest wherever you are.

Close your eyes, if that feels safe, and bring your attention to the natural rhythm of your breath. No need to change it—just notice, allow it to be what it is.

Now, take a slow inhale through your nose for a count of four . . .

Hold gently at the top for two . . .

And exhale softly through your mouth for a count of six.

Let's repeat that two more times:

Inhale for four . . . hold for two . . . exhale for six . . .

And one more . . .

Inhale . . . hold . . . exhale . . .

As you breathe, imagine each exhale releasing a layer that does not belong to your truest self.

Feel yourself softening into who you already are. When you're ready, open your eyes—or simply return your awareness to the space around you.

Now, let's begin.

INTRODUCTION

IF YOU ARE READY TO LOVE YOURSELF IN THE MOST BOLD AND BEAUTIFUL WAY POSSIBLE—WELCOME. RETURNING TO THE MOST AUTHENTIC VERSION OF YOURSELF IS WHAT THIS BOOK IS DESIGNED FOR. THIS BOOK, THE TIME INVESTED IN READING IT, AND APPLYING THE SUGGESTIONS IS ALL ABOUT YOU, MY FRIEND. THIS IS ALL FOR YOU.

It has been my dream to write a book that invites you to love yourself in a way that you haven't until now. You see, I know what it is like to walk around in my own skin without loving myself. I know the impact of years of self-judgment and self-doubt. Rising up from this limited and depressing way of being was worth all my effort, and now I invite you to dance in this world of beautiful co-creation.

Come with me on this journey, which I have presented as twelve different ways to look deep inside, to stand free on the holy ground of your being. Imagine standing on a mountaintop with your arms wide open, so courageously and fearlessly. That is the kind of feeling and scene that is yours after you drop all your self-deprecating habits and remember that you are a holy, sacred, and stunning human being. Yes, imagine walking around always aware of your essence. How amazing would that be?

Falling deeply and madly in love with another human being can be thought of as fairly commonplace and normal. But to fall in love with yourself might be considered self-centered. This book is dedicated to the SELF of you that is universal, which means the expanded you—the lovable you that is free, open, wondrous, and fully alive.

We humans are all part of the fabric of this glorious universe, ebbing and flowing, morphing with grace into an infinite number of forms; our human expression is just one possibility. We are all of one essence, all of the same energy that is arranged in the form of a human being. Quantum theory suggests that if all the space between our cells were removed, our physical form would shrink to the size of a pinhead. This reminds us that we are simply dense energy. If the theory is true, we could safely say we are not matter, but rather the movement of intelligence and the co-creative process of all that is.

Don't skip this quantum theory–based thought too quickly—it is important to grab hold of this idea and its implications. I repeat: If quantum theory is true to any degree, it means that your opinions, thoughts, and beliefs are a rock-solid influence on your creation. Why is this important? Because it will help you to understand you are not what you have believed yourself to be. ***You are essence, a beautiful essence that is informed by universal intelligence and strengthened by love.***

You are the music, not the instrument. You are the inspiration behind the masterpiece. You are the vibration of the spoken word. You are everywhere, yet not confined to your body. In essence, you are part of all that exists.

You exhale and another person inhales, it is the give-and-receive that has existed all through time. We are plugged into a universal flow, sharing a rhythm that beats our hearts. We often say that our heart beats due to our autonomic nervous system, but there is more than that. There is an intelligence that governs and guides this activity freely, never requiring anything in return. When we are in alignment with it, ease, grace, and glorious activity happen. When we forget that we are part of a universal loving essence and try to live life alone, separate from universal source and flow, we can find ourselves challenged, depressed, stuck, and struggling to put things right.

There is a very common practice that spiritual and life coaches like myself use. We will ask our clients to list what their values are and then we have them put these values in the order of importance. The last part is to ask our clients to be honest as they compare their values to their behaviors. Often, they will discover that while something might be important to them, they are not living up to that value in their life. One of my top values is to do whatever I can do to awaken people, or I could say remind them of who they are, of their divine birthright to a vast and stunning inner world, that when accessed creates a complimentary outer world. All my work, or my behavior, rallies around this value—to awaken those who are ready. Are you living your values? And if not, are you ready to start now?

This book is to remind you that your *self* is the portal to all your resources. This is most meaningful if you already believe that you are part of the fabric of life, a reflection so to speak of the full scope of beauty, genius, inspiration, and love that is who you are. But even if this is not what you believe, and you are more individualistic, meaning you do not necessarily subscribe to the idea that your inner world (including your beliefs) creates your outer world, you can still benefit from meandering through the concepts of this book. Why? Because you will have an opportunity to take a close inventory of your values and characteristics.

It might be a cliché to say that you have within yourself a vast wealth of spiritual resources. But then again, many clichés are born from reality, and this is one of them. You have full access to these resources through your inner landscape. One of my favorite quotes of all time is credited to Socrates: "To know thyself is the beginning of wisdom." This is the foundational idea that inspired me to write this book. It invigorates the very activity of my life. Over my decades it has become evident that the more I stop looking outside to measure myself against anyone or any situation and instead turn to my internal conversations, inspirations, fears, and concerns, the easier it is to transcend my limiting behaviors and beliefs. In other words, I have within me everything I need to be the person I want to be and to heal whatever is ailing me. This is also true for you.

You might get accused of being self-centered or self-absorbed, but self-absorption happens when one does not subscribe to the unity of life. What is the unity of life? It is a foundational belief that at a very deep and ethereal level we are all connected to one another. We are a beautiful tapestry. I am suggesting that I AM you and you ARE me, spiritually speaking, and in this inseparable connection we affect and impact one another, which makes your growth not only *not* selfish but *noble* because as you learn to love yourself, you become a gift to the planet, and we all benefit.

Throughout my years of coaching, I have taught with great conviction: There is no private good and, of course, the opposite must also be true: There is no private struggle. So your actions to raise your self-awareness and self-love will have an immediate and direct impact on everything and everyone around you, albeit subtly at first. The collective experience of our unconscious influences are of our ancestry, education, religious influences, personal trauma, and how we were raised with societal influences. These perspectives form a type of filter through which we see and experience our world—this is how consciousness forms our reality.

When you scroll through social media these days, you'll notice a growing chorus of voices encouraging you to stop living under the influence of others and simply *live your best life.* The younger generations especially resonate with this message: Just go and do you.

At first glance, it might seem self-centered. But in truth, they're onto something real. There is wisdom in reclaiming your agency, in choosing to honor your own path.

Still, let us be mindful not to swing the pendulum so far that we forget our interconnectedness. There is a balance. True authenticity doesn't ask us to fully disconnect; it invites us to show up more fully, for ourselves *and* for one another.

There is a sacred space in the center—a balanced place where we care for ourselves and others in ways that are whole and nontoxic. In this space you can breathe easy, remain calm, and live in gratitude for all you have.

As you reconnect with your authentic power and return to your essence, you'll begin to recognize this balance. You'll know when to set boundaries and when to open your heart. You'll know the difference—and you'll be empowered to make a difference.

Throughout this book, I will provide my reasons for the chapter headings, some words about why I included those chapters, suggestions on how to embrace new possibilities, questions to ponder, journal prompts, and some language to seduce you to look at your human self so you can experience your spiritual and sacred authentic self, unencumbered by your old habitual thinking.

You deserve to stand perfectly grounded in who you are, expressing the fullest version of who you are, which might be something that is unfamiliar. Most of us arrive clumsily into adulthood, often trying to survive our family and the conditioning of all that surrounds us. You might be aware that you did this, or you might not. It is not easy to be objective about ourselves. This is part of the journey.

I believe that as you move through the chapters of this book and apply the simple suggestions in each chapter, you will gain agency over your conditioned self, the self with the small s. *The self with the small* s *is your conditioned, ego-based self.*

Following this path will open your eyes and your heart to your beauty. If you already have a hunger for freedom from societal conditioning, good for you. If you don't, you can cultivate it as you embrace and absorb the concepts in this book.

THE PROMISE OF THIS BOOK, IF FULLY READ AND PRACTICED, IS THIS: YOU WILL SEE, FEEL, AND EMBRACE A BEAUTY AND STRENGTH THAT IS YOUR AUTHENTIC SELF.

Your spiritual authenticity is not something you have to gain or fix. Your work is to walk the spiritual path of *your* unfolding. Your spiritual authenticity is YOU; it is who you are and who you have always been. Together, let's ***get your power back, or maybe get it for the first time***.

You have within you a map of who you are and, as you reveal all your parts, you will come to know other people better because, in many ways, we share so many qualities. You have contained within your body and mind a record of pain and trauma, but you also possess all the necessary solutions. Your body was designed to heal, and if you can get out of the way and stay on the path to your inner landscape, you can unlock those healing qualities. You have it all—begin to believe that, because the more you ponder it, the more it will cultivate in you and be available to you.

There is nothing new that needs to be gathered or added to you for this healing power to work. Instead, your job is to release all thoughts of doubt and fear as you entertain a new possibility. Your spiritual authenticity is your pure essence unencumbered by the drama of the human element.

As you journey deeper into yourself, you may encounter parts of you that are asking for healing. How do you heal them? With love. Love every piece of yourself, including your missteps, triumphs, and everything that has shaped you. Be tender with your memories, kind to your past, and patient with the process. And gently release what was never truly yours to carry, although this can be difficult to identify.

At your core, there is a place that has never been hurt, harmed, or injured in any way—a space that was and always will be whole and perfect. This is the home of your spiritual authentic self—the wellspring of your purest power. It's always there, quietly guiding you beneath the noise, patiently waiting for you to recognize it, trust in it, and step into the fullness of your being.

You don't have to earn this place or prove yourself worthy of it. You already are worthy. Your existence proves your worthiness.

While my original purpose in writing this book was to celebrate the spiritual beauty of living a fully authentic life, I believe it's equally valuable to gently explore the potential impact of inauthenticity—so that we may more fully appreciate the gifts and sacred power of aligning with our true self.

THE FACE OF SPIRITUAL AUTHENTICITY

WE WANT TO LIVE AUTHENTICALLY, NOT AUTOMATICALLY. WE WANT TO CREATE BY CHOICE AND DESIGN, NOT BY DEFAULT.

Before we go any further, let us pause and turn inward to consider: What is authenticity, truly? And why is it sacred? To live authentically is to align with the indwelling Spirit, to honor the Divine blueprint etched within us. It is not something we become—it is who we already are beneath the layers we've been conditioned to wear. As an author and a teacher, I cannot take you where I have not traveled myself, so I will share pieces of my personal journey while inviting you to find your own path home (to your authentic self). Along the way I will challenge you gently, hoping to spark new ideas and a willingness to journey with me.

Because knowing myself is one of my greatest values, it is my regular practice to question everything about my life: my motivation and temptation to avoid things, and in general what makes me—me. This drives all my teachings and who I am. In truth, I was sick and tired of being sick and tired. I couldn't stand living in fear anymore; I had to do something about it. It took years before I would learn to live fearlessly, but it was worth the effort.

Most humans walking the planet do not really know who they are, why they do what they do, or what is actually motivating their lives. It is not a simple or obvious thing to decide to dive into self-understanding. It is a critical life-altering decision that requires true courage.

Until we make the conscious choice to wake up, we move through life like conditioned robots, interacting and behaving according to the domestication programmed into us by our families, friends, educational systems, religious leaders, and the marketing monsters that have mastered the science of triggering dopamine drips to capture our attention and manipulate our desires.

To be authentic, we have to peel away years of conditioning—some things are obvious, but there is much more that is not. While you might think you know why you like that chocolate cake with almond filling and ganache frosting, you most likely don't. You also probably don't *really* know why you're attracted to a redhead, jock, delicate woman, businessman, or someone who displays tattoos and piercings.

You might think that I am exaggerating, but I am not. The infinite number of things that influence you started before you were born. That which has helped to form you started when your grandmother or great-grandmother survived the Great Depression, and her fear of lack left a trail of fear in those who came after her, but neither you nor your mother might know why you feel better when your pantry is full. Fear of not being able to feed you and your siblings traumatized your mother, and she acted from and made choices because of that trauma, even though she did not experience it directly.

Your mother inherited fear without a full measure of understanding why. Your mother and father adopted many fears from your grandparents, but they just thought they were being frugal. While they never knew true hunger, the fear of that experience was living in the cells of their bodies and continued to influence them.

I invite you to take time to value the influences of your ancestors and also forgive them for some of these influences. Just as generational wealth is handed down, so, too, are generational biases, fears, and prejudices that are quite challenging to recognize.

As you begin this journey, let yourself be curious about all your motivating factors. In this moment, without needing to fix or figure anything out, what do you sense is most true about who you are beneath the surface?

Use a journal or blank sheet of paper and let your pen move without judgment to answer that question, and please allow your soul to speak freely.

This is our path to home—our authenticity . . .

Let us take a quiet moment to explore why this path matters and the radiant gifts it holds for the soul. When we begin to glimpse the blessings that unfold along the way, the journey becomes not only worthwhile but also profoundly moving. Think of it as a reset. I'll share with you that I like me much more than I once did, and I walk around way more confidently than I once did. I wanted freedom and I discovered this was the way to get it.

My intention is simple: to share what I've come to know through my own unfolding, and to walk beside you as we each find our way back to the heart of who we truly are. As Ram Dass so lovingly reminded us, "We are all just walking each other home."

May this shared journey be one of gentle remembrance, where we breathe deeply, love freely, and awaken—again and again—to the truth of our being.

For now, take a gentle pause.

Take a slow, mindful breath. Place your hand on your heart, if that feels comfortable. Ask yourself, without needing an answer right away: What does "home" feel like within me?

Let that question rest quietly in your heart as we continue.

What does it take to be authentic?

To be authentic—truly authentic—you must heal your insecurities, learn to love and accept yourself completely, and take time to deconstruct the masks that are your public face. I will be asking you hundreds of questions. As you learn to identify the things that need healing, inquire within and set a plan to liberate what needs to be released.

You are here to walk naked into the light of love and intelligence—metaphorically naked, of course—or not. That's up to you. Along this path you will have the opportunity to journey with your pure, spiritually ordained essence. As you expand your sense of awe and curiosity, you will find your hidden treasures.

To be authentic is to embrace your vulnerability—which might initially scare the crap out of you. Don't confuse vulnerability with weakness; they are totally different. Vulnerability is about living in life without arming or defending yourself. You will learn that having strength and certainty of purpose is not the only way to be. You can be strong and gentle. To accept your vulnerability is to remove the masks you wear and to be willing to be seen as you are, not as you project yourself to be.

One of my greatest influences is Ernest Holmes, a spiritual teacher and the author of *The Science of Mind*, a classic of metaphysical teaching. One of my favorite quotes from the book is this: "Create or perish." So, together, we shall create—boldly, brilliantly, beautifully, and definitely.

Part of this journey will be about taking an inventory of your values, committing to those values, and then acting accordingly even when it is not convenient, even when it hurts. It is important that you do take time to honor yourself, the lessons you have already learned, and the resulting richness of life.

To be authentic you must learn to practice radical self-honesty. It is a beautiful thing to learn to be honest about your emotions, and to learn how to identify your physical reactions so you can in turn learn from them. Some emotions are obvious and some are very subtle. Learning how to identify any of them will give you an advantage of knowing exactly who you are. (This is the somatic aspect of this journey. Pay close attention to the messages of your body temple.)

When you embrace your authenticity, you will want to learn to admit when you're wrong about almost anything and take responsibility when you make a mistake or find yourself being judgmental or prejudiced. One of the most freeing things I have learned in my life came with being able to admit when I was wrong or when I screwed up and made a bad decision. Being able to admit my errors allowed me to get ahead of feeling embarrassed, guilty, or ashamed. In the end it is quite freeing.

When you are authentic you will be able to embrace your imperfections without compounding them with self-judgment and self-criticisms. We are all imperfect, or we can say we are all perfect in our imperfections—a paradox, yes, but a very real one. When you are willing to love yourself as you are, life becomes more loving and gentler. When you know this, your authenticity might soften you, but it will *never* weaken you.

Being fully embraced will leave you metaphorically naked in your spiritual authority as you gain the ability to love life in the most glorious ways possible. You will learn to admire and embrace the little things, the small miracles, the acts of kindness that might be barely perceptible to the conditioned mind. To the one who has taken time to strip away their conditioning, beauty and kindness are revealed around every corner. Being authentic in this way opens you to being fully present in the moment.

This new way of being paves the way for spontaneous moments of joy. The kind that come from seeing a sunrise, sharing a warm hug, or hearing a baby laugh. This actually might be the most stunning reward for regaining your authentic grounding. I was walking in a beautiful rainforest in the US state of Washington, and the sights, sounds, and even the fragrances erupted through me as tears of joy.

BE AUTHENTIC ON YOUR TERMS

As you read, contemplate, and practice the offerings in this book, let's make one point very clear: You must feel free to *give yourself permission to hide*. I'll explain as we go further.

I'm certain this sounds contrary, but it is important to trust your intuition. Being authentic and being able to show up authentically does not require you to share your deepest secrets or even your ponderances with anybody—and most certainly not if you don't feel safe. As the saying goes, you get to *do* you *on your own terms*.

The gift of authenticity is to find yourself free from feeling compelled by anyone else to reveal what you might not be ready to share. Wisdom must be applied here, of course, as choice is the gift of being authentic and self-confident. It is the wisdom to not cast pearls before swine, to not put yourself in harm's way, and to not put yourself in the hands of someone who does not share your spiritual worldview.

While I support all humans in becoming more conscious, the reality is that a great majority of our global population is not conscious. These individuals might even feel threatened by the power you display as you embrace your personal power. Yes, when you are strong and confident, you don't have to care about getting approval but you might decide to not engage with others who cannot meet you along this path. That is your prerogative. So I repeat: *GIVE YOURSELF PERMISSION TO HIDE OR WITHHOLD ON YOUR TERMS, while knowing that discretion is wisdom.*

This was one of the most valuable lessons I learned along my journey. If I have piqued your interest, we can walk together.

TO BE AUTHENTIC

To be authentic is to be naked.
To be authentic is to speak one's heart.
To be authentic is to live out loud.
To be authentic is to love the being of your choice.
To be authentic is to never again make an excuse for being you.
To be authentic is to touch that place of power that is your birthright.
To be authentic is to be comfortable in your own skin, never wanting to be anything other than who you are.

THE SHADOWS OF INAUTHENTICITY

FRUSTRATION COMES FROM NOT KNOWING THE DANCE STEPS.

UNTIL YOU WAKE UP AND REMEMBER WHO YOU ARE, YOU WILL BE CONSTANTLY CREATING FROM WHAT ALREADY WAS, WITHOUT AN ORIGINAL THOUGHT.

With each step you take, it is important to understand the subtle and grand signs and issues that show up when we live life as a conditioned robot rather than as our authentic self. Most of us are familiar with "unpleasant" emotions like persistent anxiety, lingering sadness, or a vague sense that something is missing. Now you can use unpleasant emotions to help you gently navigate your way back to your authentic self. I encourage you to find relief in knowing that these challenges are not personal flaws to be fixed but an invitation to return home.

When we stray too far from the truth of who we are—often without even realizing it because of our early programming—we may begin to feel anxious, have low energy, or feel restless or deeply unfulfilled. These feelings are not signs of failure or weakness. They are sacred signals—messengers inviting us back to ourselves. Please know that it is human nature to unconsciously adopt the habits that cause inauthentic behaviors.

They were all created by our ego so we could manage our struggles. They each exist as a survival mechanism. Your ego works for you on your behalf.

Consider how exhausting it is to constantly walk around while wearing an uncomfortable, ill-fitting mask to hide the parts of you that you have tried to reject. Accepting that you wear a mask or masks, you may be able to identify some of the other coping mechanisms you created. They were most likely unconsciously self-created so you could feel acceptable while you were hiding. Just how much energy does it take to hide the parts of you that you think of as unworthy? Again, IT IS EXHAUSTING.

A PERSONAL NOTE HERE

While I was writing this book, my husband was diagnosed with cancer. Not a day went by without my needing to pay close attention to how I was showing up. It was a constant mental battle to decide just how honest I should be when caring people would ask me how I was or how he was. What does authentic expression sound like under these conditions? Am I required to spill my guts? Was it OK to give an affirmative answer—so the person inquiring could feel better while I discouraged further inquiry?

I will tell you very honestly, the answer is this: His health status remains a moving target, and I do my best to express myself without denying my emotions as the journey continues.

I cannot repeat this point often enough. Living inauthentically is energy zapping and a denial of your fullest potential, all while being emotionally and mentally exhausting. It might be difficult to recognize this because most people live inauthentically all the time without realizing it. It seems normal to hide or attempt to compensate for aspects of yourself that you have been quietly criticizing for years. Most likely, you are familiar with that part of you that judges yourself for how you look, for your intelligence or the lack thereof, for marrying the person of your dreams and then divorcing after a year, for having children that are challenging, for not pursuing a degree that could have made all the difference in the world.

Every time you have ever judged yourself, you also quietly shunned that part of you, which becomes a shadow part. But in hiding that part, you have become what you are not. Hear that again.

In hiding your negative, self-denigrating voice, you became what you are not. And because of your dislike for these parts, you begin to twist yourself into the proverbial pretzel in an attempt to function despite the dysfunction.

This attempt to compensate for our perceived limitations is so commonplace that it almost seems natural. In the less aware mind, it can also seem like a logical thing to do—yes, it might seem logical to try to make up for what you *think* is not acceptable about yourself. For example, if you're trying to be the smart one in the room because you feel unintelligent, you might toss unfounded facts about, or you might try to be the funny one in the room to get attention, or spend money on things that you don't need so you can impress onlookers who don't even care about you. These are all futile efforts to hide but they all live in our inauthenticity.

You might think that hiding those parts you don't like and creating new parts you think you do like are ways toward raising your self-image, but I assure you if you attempt to be what you are not without loving all aspects of your life, you will never feel complete, whole, well—or authentic. One aspect of this is pretense.

THE INNER TEXTURE OF INAUTHENTICITY

Let's take a gentle, curious look at some of the ways inauthenticity can show up as shadow in our lives. The purpose of this investigation is to recognize the warning signs.

As you read through this section, I invite you to reflect with kindness—not judgment—on your own journey. You may recognize some of these patterns in yourself, perhaps without ever having named them before. If so, let that recognition be a moment of empowerment, not shame. **This is not a checklist of faults—it's an invitation to greater awareness and motivation for the work ahead.**

One of the first signs of living inauthentically is low self-esteem. It often reflects a deep, unspoken exhaustion from constantly pretending to be someone you're not. And let me say this clearly: This is *almost never* a conscious choice. Most of us are simply doing our best to navigate the world, to survive within the illusion of what we've been told is "normal." Later in the book, we'll dive into both self-esteem and self-worth as separate and vital areas of focus—because they are that important.

We'll also go deeper into the identity crisis of feeling like a fraud—a silent ache that so many carry. When we lose touch with our true self, we often find ourselves asking, "Who am I really?" Walking through life inauthentically is like wearing a mask you forgot you put on. You pretend to be what you think others need or expect, all while hiding what's real. How exhausting—and how absurd—that we try to do this so often. Even putting on a brave face when we are actually afraid or struggling is a quiet act of self-denial. It seems small, but over time, it chips away at our sense of self.

The effort to maintain a facade often leads to chronic stress and burnout. Pretending takes a lot of energy, more than you can imagine. You might find yourself feeling inexplicably tired or depleted without knowing why. That's because your personality, especially when it's not aligned with your truth, is like a fire that needs constant fuel to keep burning. Maintaining an image of who you think you're supposed to be consumes energy in ways we don't always recognize.

Have you noticed that when you build relationships from that inauthentic place, those relationships tend to lack depth and real connection? Relationships rooted in pretense are often transactional or conditional, and over time, they become unfulfilling and even painful. The cost of these shallow connections is high—namely, the loss of ourselves and the erosion of our core values. Think of how many politicians function in this way: always performing, rarely revealing what's real. And consider this: How much do you trust them?

What's even more curious about the human experience is how often we sabotage ourselves in subtle ways. We make decisions—sometimes unconsciously—that shape our lives, and when the results don't align with our truth, we feel resentful. But often, the resentment isn't aimed at the world—it's directed inward. We resent ourselves for having created something we no longer want, even though we did it with the best survival instincts we had at the time.

Inauthenticity also takes a toll on the body. Chronic stress, anxiety, and emotional disconnection often manifest as physical symptoms: headaches, fatigue, muscle tension, or even immune system challenges. Your body, unlike your mind, doesn't lie. It tells the truth through sensation, pain, and imbalance. Part of the journey toward authenticity is learning how to listen to the body's messages and respond with care.

Without authenticity, life can feel aimless. When you're not centered in your truth, it's difficult to recognize your passions or purpose. You might find yourself constantly looking outward for approval or trying to fit into places that don't feel right. You may follow others, hoping they'll lead you to yourself, only to feel more disconnected and lost.

All of this leads to a quiet, smoldering unhappiness. Living inauthentically doesn't usually end in a dramatic collapse—it results in a steady, silent sense that something is missing. And in truth, something *is* missing: you. The you that was born to be free, expressive, vibrant, joyful, and beautifully alive.

So as you walk through the pages of this book, do so with wonder, curiosity, and boldness as your companions. Those qualities will help you stay open when it's tempting to shut down, and remain soft when old patterns ask you to harden. As you gently strip away the layers between your conditioned self and your authentic self, something beautiful will begin to rise. Joy will find you in simple, unexpected ways. Laughter will bubble up from places you had forgotten existed. Love will return—not just from others, but from within.

And please remember: You deserve all of it. Every bit.

KEEPING ME HONEST AND KEEPING IT REAL

Because I can never live outside the work I teach or the books I write, I am constantly impacted by my own efforts to rise above the conditions I face, as I've already shared with you about my husband. This is a difficult standard to maintain, but a worthy one. It keeps me honest. Only when I've determined something is good enough to share will I teach it to others. I cannot take you down a dark path of discovery unless I am holding the light of revelation. This journey cannot be faked. I must be demonstrating the concepts in my own life before I am free to talk and teach about them.

So if you are wondering whether or not I do the work or if I have felt lost, confused, and at times helpless, to these questions I answer yes. This work has been part of my life's journey, but my focus on authenticity has been heightened since writing this book. As I started writing, I would get stopped in my tracks to reflect upon my own life and ask myself, "Am I actualizing that which I'm sharing with you?" And I'll be honest with you: There were times when I was not.

I always take a break to reflect back on my own behavior and my decisions. All of this leads me to asking some version of this question over and over again: "Am I being authentic?" There is a plethora of questions that I've learned to ask myself that might seem obvious to someone who lives authentically, but for me—and if you're anything like me—it's possible these questions might jar your reality as they have mine.

Here are some questions I ask to keep myself honest:

* Am I actually doing what I want to do right now?
* Am I working in a career that fills my soul?
* Do I really want to cook dinner tonight?
* Do I want to be the one who entertains my family for every holiday?
* Do I really want to go to that wedding or that baptism or that retirement party?
* Am I behaving in ways that are commensurate with things that sing my soul or am I playing small?

Do any of those resonate with you? What questions can you ask yourself to shake up your current reality with the intention of returning to your authentic place of power?

These are not small or simple questions. When answered honestly, they are deeply profound questions. Try whispering these questions to yourself and feel into your reaction. When I began asking myself the first question, I was jarred when the answer was no. I discovered that I was living most of my life as an automaton, going through the motions with no thought or feeling. Nothing is further from what I want for my life than living on automatic. My personal desire and my desire for you, my dear reader, is that you open to being the unpredictable you, born of your heart's desire and need to express the all of you—the unique you that only you can be.

Approximately two years before writing this book, I resigned as the spiritual director of a center that I had led for twenty-five years. Why? Because I was not fulfilled. I left with my faith intact but without a true plan for my future. But then miraculously, as I said *no* to living inauthentically, I simultaneously decided to live while expressing my authentic self, and this book is now one of three volumes that I have penned in that time. Being an author and a teacher full-time fills my soul. So, as I dove into the opportunity to test the waters of being authentic, a world of possibilities opened up. I took my own advice and I have chosen to be my dream.

SUPER BOWL SUNDAY

Here is a silly example but one that will show you a deeper truth of how simply we can sacrifice our authentic self. It was Super Bowl Sunday, we had friends over, I made a bunch of appetizers, sat and watched football, and had a great time. But my friends who were going to be leaving soon felt compelled to get up and start cleaning my kitchen before I felt ready to do so. Numerous times I said to them, "Please don't do that, just take home whatever you want to take with you, I'll clean up the rest later." Why did I do this? I did it because, in that moment, I didn't want to get up out of obligation and participate when I wasn't ready. I actually sat there in my chair watching the end of the game and the celebration, asking myself if I was being true to myself right now. And the answer was YES, absolutely, I wanted to sit there and finish watching the game. And so I did.

Sounds like a piece of cake? Not so fast. This brought up additional questions inside my mind and made me wonder what my friends thought about me not getting up when they got up. Did they think I'm selfish or that I'm lazy? As I heard these questions whirling around inside my head, I recognized my need to be liked and get approval, and I was not interested in feeding that mental addiction. I just wanted to do what I wanted to do in that moment—without explaining myself to anyone. I chose to embrace my authentic self at that moment as I took that risk. Being who you are will call you to take risks. It will be scary. It will be worth it. Again, this is a simple example of a deeper issue.

Let's take a closer look at these inner dynamics. As you read, see if any part of this resonates with your own experience.

In so doing, I felt a quiet joy arise within me—because I had chosen to please my soul, not perform for acceptance. This is my dream for you, sweet reader.

This choice became a "win" in my mind that I would nurture. I gave myself permission to be fully, freely me. And something beautiful unfolded: The people around me felt that freedom, too. When *you* decide to be *you*—authentically and unapologetically—you create space for others to do the same. This kind of freedom is reciprocal. It flows both ways. Freedom to be you creates an automatic invitation for others to be free.

FOMO NO MORE

I have many reasons to be doing this work, so I will share with you a bit more insight into my actual motivation. I have never blended well into new groups—or even familiar ones for that matter. Add this to the fact that I am an introvert, I used to have a gross lack of self-confidence, and I was always needing other peoples' approval. It wasn't exactly a great recipe for being a confident woman walking in the world with my head held high.

> ***We ask ourselves, who am I to be brilliant, gorgeous, talented, fabulous? Actually, who are you not to be? You are a child of God. Your playing small doesn't serve the world. There's nothing enlightened about shrinking so that other people won't feel insecure around you.***
>
> **—MARIANNE WILLIAMSON**

It wasn't until I truly embraced the fact that I am an introvert that I found peace in attending professional meetings and conferences. At these events, my friends and colleagues would often gather for a drink or a bite to eat after the day's busyness. Sometimes I would feel too awkward to bow out, so I would say yes to go along just to fit in and suffer through it. But when I finally claimed my introversion, I gave myself permission to say *no*—to not go along just to fit in. In doing so, I found freedom. I no longer forced myself into social situations that caused stress and anxiety in my life.

I love how society has identified this way of being: FOMO (which stands for fear of missing out). I used to have a bad case of it, but now I am fully cured.

This is truly a great example of how things can change when you walk this path courageously back to your authentic self and your power. You stop doing things to please others, you stop doing things to get approval, and you most definitely stop doing things to be right. I cannot tell you the peace of mind that I found after I started saying no: no to invitations, no to going out for a drink, no to being around a particular group of people that I didn't really want to be with. Was my world, my social world, smaller because of that? Yep, and I'm so much happier for it.

Sometimes the inspiration to do things differently can come from the most unexpected places. During one of my late-night Facebook scrolls, I came upon a post where the individual was speaking about how most of us are not now and never will live a life that is authentic or unique because most of us live on unconscious repeat.

The point this person was trying to make is that we live a very conditioned and repetitive life. This is partially due to the neural pathways we have created in our brains through repetition. Most of what we do every day is based on what we did the day before, the week before, the month before, the year before, and decades prior. I started to think about traditions that we have in my family, and I started pondering whether or not those traditions still held value for me. Did I want to commit to them indefinitely? Now I will tell you, some of them I'm very attached to because they are a suture, pulling a thread of familiarity through the years of memories of my children growing and now my grandchildren. But there is another side of me that has come to realize that, often, even my holiday celebrations are habits based on an old reality.

Turkey No More

Here's a funny little truth bomb: Every Thanksgiving, I have to admit it all over again. I don't like turkey, not even a little bit. So why am I eating it? Why am I roasting it, basting it, dressing it up like it's the main event when I'd rather skip straight to the sides? Every year I say, "I'm just here for the fixings," and guess what? So does half the table.

So why the turkey trauma? Why the annual poultry production? It's like I inherited the hypnosis, then turned around and passed it down like some kind of casserole cult leader.

Now, you might think I'm being dramatic—and maybe I am—but **here's what I know about habits: The ones we don't question are the ones that quietly run our lives**. They put us on autopilot. And how in the world can we be authentic if we're out here living like robots?

What I'm about to offer may not be practical if you are busy raising your family or trying to keep your business afloat with people depending on you, but even within those realities, there's room to shift, to stop repeating old patterns, and to open ourselves to new possibilities—not based on fashion or social media trends, but from our heart. What if we made a practice of connecting with our heart every day, asking ourselves questions that could shake us free from our conditioned experience that led us back to the free, authentic version of ourselves?

Imagine, at the start of your day, you ask this question into the universal construct and truly open yourself to the answer: "How could I experience today if I followed my heart and made choices that were true to my heart, instead of living from a place of conditioning?"

What if I let go of all the "have tos" and embraced the "want tos"? How would my life change? What if I ate when I was hungry, not when the clock told me to? What if I said *no* instead of saying *yes* out of pressure?

These are small questions that have the power to jar us out of autopilot.

Yes, if you have responsibilities and obligations, it's not always possible to change everything overnight. But even within those responsibilities, there's space for you to be you. For example, you might not feel like serving meat and potatoes for dinner (yes, that is an old concept); maybe you want to serve breakfast food for dinner instead. You might not want to make your bed every day, or maybe you don't want to sit in the same spot at the table each time you eat. All habits should be examined.

Wherever we get caught in habits, we are in danger of being unconscious.

There's freedom in the small choices we make every day. The key is to begin asking, to start questioning the default, and to find the room to express your true self, even amid the routines that fill your day.

ROOTS BEFORE WINGS—THE TOOLS LAID OUT . . .

Here is a brief explanation of the tools included along each path, but first a story about how important training and practices are when you want to become an expert at something. About thirty-five years ago, I made a decision to give back to society in a meaningful way. I chose to train as an EMT—an emergency medical technician. The training was rigorous and intense, laced with the stress of knowing that this was truly life-or-death work.

The journey began with first aid and CPR certifications for administering on both adults and children. From there, I continued into full EMT training at the local hospital. Before we were even allowed out into the field, we had to volunteer many hours in the emergency room—just to get our feet wet.

In the ER, we were allowed to take blood pressure readings and interact with a few patients, but mostly we watched and learned. The focus was on observation, humility, and teamwork.

We trained for everything, such as how to drive the ambulance, how to operate lifesaving equipment, how to read the signs of trauma or distress, and how to work seamlessly with other responders. The training seemed endless, and that was intentional. You had to be ready for anything.

WOMAN WHO DIED

One day, we were called to the home of a woman who, by all outward appearances, was the picture of health—before we arrived, that is—a forty-year-old, tennis-playing mom living a vibrant life. But that day, she came home from tennis, laid down for a nap, and never woke up. By the time we arrived, she had already been gone for several minutes. Her husband was in complete anguish, calling her name with the most bloodcurdling screams I've ever heard.

That day, I learned the true value of training—not just the technical skills, but the ability to remain grounded and clear in the middle of emotional chaos. While her husband cried out in heartbreak, we moved her to the floor and began CPR. The law required us to attempt lifesaving measures even though her body appeared lifeless. I found myself kneeling beside her, performing chest compressions, staying in sync with my fellow volunteers, and communicating calmly with the medics as they arrived.

I was calm. I was focused. I was present. And I knew exactly what to do. Why? Because I had trained thoroughly.

I'm sorry to tell you that she did not survive. This is not a story of miraculous recovery. But it *is* a story about the power of preparation, practice, and presence. About what it means to cultivate the skills you need *before* you're in the middle of crisis or chaos.

And that, in essence, is why I share this story with you now—because the practices and habits in this book are like your own inner EMT training. They're here to support you in developing inner stability, clarity, and the ability to respond—not react—when life gets intense.

When you're face-to-face with a challenge—when emotions are high, and the stakes feel real—you won't have to stop and think. You'll know what to do. Your new way of being will already be alive in you. You'll recognize the old pattern, hear the voice of doubt, and *choose* something different. That's when true transformation takes root.

Over time, you'll begin to notice a shift. You'll stop tolerating the voice of negativity in your head. You'll interrupt the inner critic before it even finishes its sentence. You'll stop judging yourself, because eventually it will become clear that your self-judgment is unnecessary, counterproductive, and untrue.

You'll begin to expect more of yourself—not from pressure or perfectionism, but from love. And through that loving standard, you'll grow in self-acceptance, compassion, worthiness, and inner power. Each leg of this journey will introduce you to new tools and insights. These tools are designed to meet you exactly where you are, help you recognize your potential, and support you through the blocks and challenges that arise along the way. This is no surface-level path. This is deep, profound soul work.

My approach to teaching is to begin by helping people deconstruct their current thinking. To gently break apart what they *think* they know, so they can make room for something new. Because let's be honest: If a teacup is already full, you can't pour anything more into it. It just spills everywhere and makes a mess.

The same goes for the mind. An open mind is an available one.

So, becoming an open vessel—curious, spacious, willing—is the first and most powerful step toward real growth. This is the time to set your intention to be courageously free.

I'm genuinely excited for you. I say that because I remember what it felt like when I first began breaking free from the confines of old, limiting beliefs. There were parts of me buried beneath fear and doubt—parts I hadn't seen in years. And to reclaim my grounded, authentic self? That has been one of the greatest gifts of my life.

Now, let me say something that may sound bold: You might not like my authentic self. And others might not like yours. That's OK. One of the most liberating lessons I've ever learned is this: **Stop waiting for the approval of others.** Learning these new tools and skills will help you to find comfort with yourself so completely, your self-approval will no longer depend upon the acceptance of another—that is freedom, true freedom.

The goal of this work is not to get more people to like you more, or for people to like you more. This journey is about you liking and approving of yourself and feeling completely comfortable in your own skin.

We are not here to conform. We are not here to twist ourselves into knots to fit someone else's mold. We are here to become who we truly are. Learning new skills and developing new thinking habits will get you there.

Here, now, are the tools and their descriptions so you can properly prepare for what you will be asked to do. **This book contains twelve chapters, each one I consider to be a "path" that will bring you more awareness of yourself, and more internal power.** Each of the paths we will travel in this book will have a quote that offers you wisdom from an inclusive set of teachers. These offerings are of the ages and some current wisdom teachers. An important part of growing is learning to find value in other teachers and teachings. Stretch your mind, my friend.

Each chapter will then have a **description of the path**, not according to any dictionary, but according to how I teach. This will clue you into my teaching style, so you know what to expect in each section, and this will lead to a quick start, which will help you get started right away. I enjoy my beingness, but I also enjoy my doingness and can be impatient to get started at times. Enjoy these suggestions. They will offer you a jump-start, but don't make the assumption that they can replace what's in the chapter—they can't.

The main part of each chapter will be **the teaching**. This is the section where I presume to know something that you might not. Arrogant maybe, but my offering is based solely on my personal journey and how I have gone about teaching from this journey and all my experiences.

And of course, what is knowledge without action and practices? Also in each chapter I will offer you some **additional how-tos**. I do like making things clear and simple, and so providing you with some practices is my way of doing that. All of life is a mystery but the path to walk along should not be. I prefer a well-lit, well-paved path of proven principles. And I consider them proven because I have used them, suggested them in my coaching and classes, and seen the amazing results in my life and others' lives.

Neville Goddard, an elder master spiritual teacher said, "Imagination is another word for God." While *god* might not be in your vernacular, intelligence and co-creative energy *is* flowing all around you; and to the degree that you are able to imagine your desired outcome, you are able to actualize it. So, in each section, I ask you to ***imagine with me***, because it is through imagination that we create.

This journey is about uncovering your inner wisdom, and one of the best ways to accomplish this is through creative writing. So, you will be offered ***journal prompts*** to express your bounty of wisdom and self-knowledge, but if you are an artist, feel free to draw or doodle if that serves you, or if you are a composer, write music.

There is something special to my heart, a spiritual practice that I learned that was inspired by renowned spiritual teacher Ernest Holmes. I have renamed the practice ***spiritual mindshift***, and it is one of the most important aspects of this journey. Spiritual mindshifts seep into places within, where nothing else can go, and they will support you in renewing your way of being in the most loving and gentle way. I have created spiritual mindshift scripts for each path, and there are extras in the back of the book.

I have included some instructions in the back of this book so you can learn to be more confident in speaking or writing your own spiritual mindshifts. Look under: "Mindshift: Speaking the Language of Your Heart."

Learning how to speak to yourself in a meaningful way is not as simple as it sounds. For that reason, I have designed ***letters to the self*** as one of the more self-loving practices there is, especially if you allow yourself the freedom to drink in the words and let them settle in you like a soft summer mist. Read these letters before going to sleep or upon waking in the morning. These are the two times of day when your mind is most open to influence.

I offer you ***affirmations*** to use throughout your days. Think of these affirmations that I have provided more like mantras that you keep handy for when you need to shift your mind and heart. You will be invited to change your thinking habits, and having these affirmations or mantras available will be a great reminder during those moments when fear or doubt might creep in.

And to round it out, I included a short reminder to **breathe** through the practices. This is an important step because you will benefit from growing your somatic awareness, and I close out each chapter with **pearls of wisdom** from each chapter.

Lastly, if you are a coach, spiritual practitioner, or a therapist, you will find that I make reference to exercises that you can use with your clients, though this whole book can be used for that purpose. Remember, our goal as any kind of helper/healer is to promote self-awareness for our clients. Wherever you see journal prompts, exercises, or affirmations, use them to expand the growth of the people under your care.

Things to Ponder

Within these pages, you'll find invitations, questions, and reflections to guide your journey inward. You are encouraged to contemplate, journal, and, most importantly, listen for the quiet wisdom already within you.

- How do I begin to uncover my authentic self when the layers of conditioning are so thick and blinding?
- How can I walk with clarity and confidence, even when I don't yet understand the roots of my patterns or preferences?
- What beauty, joy, or sacred truth might I have been overlooking due to my own unawareness?

LET'S GO HOME

Here we go, fellow traveler. Let's go on a wild danceathon together into the heart of the book, the soul of the journey. Let's lead each other into the middle of the dance floor where life is juicy and wonderfully alive. These next chapters are not just words on a page; they are invitations to dance through your life. Each one is a path, leading you back to yourself. Let's go with determined minds, like best friends who are ready and willing to try anything and go anywhere for a great adventure.

As you stroll—or dance!—down each path, I invite you to bring an open mind, willing heart, and childlike curiosity. Some ideas may feel familiar, some may feel new, and some may even stir discomfort. If that happens, don't turn away. **Let your reaction be a doorway, not a dead end.** Fear, resistance, and even irritation are not signs to stop. They are signs to lean in and look deeper.

I've chosen twelve specific focuses to guide this process. Could there be more? Of course. But in our often busy, overcommitted lives, I wanted to offer something that is accessible and doable while still being powerful.

Take your time, read slowly, and embody the teaching completely. This is a cross-country road trip, not just a short stroll across town. It's a sacred and exciting unfolding, a personal pilgrimage.

A cross-country road trip is like a marathon that requires the entirety of the runner to be trained. Marathon runners not only train for physical endurance but they also train for the mental resolve to make it past "the wall," which is the name they give for the twentieth mile—a breakthrough that all marathoners must face before they finish at 26.2 miles.

As I suggested earlier in the book, consider reading this with a friend or in a small group. Sharing this experience allows you to speak your truth, hear others, and hold space for one another when old habits try to shut down new insights. Connection is part of the medicine.

Although there's no single "right" order to follow—each path offers its own gifts—path 1 begins with self-talk. Your inner voice is the narrator of your life, and if that voice doesn't change, no outer transformation will truly stick. The way you speak to yourself determines how you move through every other path in this book.

From there, let your intuition guide you. Meander. Linger. Return to chapters more than once. **Let this book be a conversation, not a checklist.**

But most of all, make it playful. Make it yours. **Let this be an exploration, not an obligation.** This is not therapy; it's not a test. This is a journey of becoming. A return to your fully ordained self: beautiful, joyful, strong, and wonderfully alive.

Welcome to the journey. Welcome to the practice. Welcome to the Sacred Return as together we dance like nobody's watching.

Are you ready?

1

RECLAIMING THE LANGUAGE OF THE INNER VOICE

Your Dance with Self-Talk

Your mind is a powerful thing. When you filter it with positive thoughts, your life will start to change.

—GAUTAMA BUDDHA

Description of Self-Talk

Self-talk is the internal dialogue that occurs within our minds, as it guides our thoughts, beliefs, and actions. It's the ongoing conversation we have with ourselves, shaping our perception of the world and our place in it. When directed positively, this inner voice can be a powerful tool for motivation, self-assurance, and resilience.

Here Is a Quick Start Option

Tune in to your inner conversation and be extremely selective about what you say to yourself and about yourself. Cultivate the discipline to make conscious choices to make sure that everything you think is self-affirming. If you catch something contrary to this, gently start

> *again. No criticism. Be kind to yourself every moment of every day*—no exceptions.

Why does this journey toward authenticity begin with self-talk? Because your internal dialogue, unwatched and undisciplined, has been working either against you or for you, throughout your entire life. It is highly likely that you were never encouraged to either monitor or discipline it. Why? Because most people have no clue that this is happening in their minds; or that their incessant thinking has actual impact.

The whole journey starts with paying equal attention to your inner and outer dialogue. This journey must begin here, because your inner dialogue is incessant. It is the most important conversation that we will have on this journey. Those quiet, barely perceptible inner whisperings will start to transform, making you focus your attention on who you have come here to be, not how easily you have given up your authentic power in the past.

Going forward for the rest of this reading, pay very close attention to your mind chatter, your reactions, and how you find yourself feeling about what is said. Getting to know yourself is the single most important path to your authentic self.

I could almost guarantee you a predictable outcome should you choose to take on the practice of monitoring your inner voice. If this is the only habit you change—if you learn to listen clearly and redirect your attention and habits of your thinking—your life will begin to flourish within weeks of a steady diet of practicing healthy self-talk. That is how important it is. You will begin to speak to yourself and about yourself in a way that raises you up.

Another important point to remember: Your inner voice is only partially yours. You have unconsciously adopted the voice of the planet, a cacophony of voices that have made their way into your thinking and subconsciousness. Very specifically you have adopted and acted upon the likes, dislikes, fears, doubts, and judgments of your family. When you are young, you have no idea that you have the option to agree or disagree, so you simply adopt. Your adult inner voice greatly reflects the conversations you heard as a child.

Unless you were fortunate enough to grow up in a conscious, self-aware household, chances are you've been subjected to the mass hypnosis of not-enoughness. Sad, but true. Are we at the mercy of this conditioning? Absolutely not. But it *does* require us to wake up, deepen our self-awareness, and expand our consciousness.

WE ARE NEVER AT THE MERCY OF WHAT WAS—NOT NOW, NOT EVER. BUT CHOOSING A NEW PATH TAKES INTENTION, AND YES, IT TAKES EFFORT.

Fortunately for some, and very unfortunately for many, **the outer voices that became your inner voice belonged to individuals who were reflecting how they felt about themselves—not how they truly saw you**. This is how our shadow is created and then projected onto others. For example, your mom, in a frustrated moment, called you stupid, but in reality, her criticism is a reflection of how she feels about herself. But your young mind was defenseless and didn't know this yet, and so you adopted this idea as truth. Let's not blame Mom, as she was repeating what was done to her. Our journey here together is to break that pattern and do better.

We label the world through the lens of our worldview, and your mind naturally seeks evidence to support what it already believes. For example, if you think the world is hard and mean, you will seek evidence to support that idea.

Because you loved your mother, your father, and your other caretakers, you trusted them. You believed what they said to you, and even what they said about you to others. When we're that young, we don't yet have the ability to discern between life-affirming truth and life-limiting stories. We simply absorb it all. We take it in as if it were gospel.

And from that fertile, impressionable soil, our self-concept begins to grow. Hopefully, I have already convinced you how important this first leg of our journey is.

That inner voice can easily go unnoticed until you make the conscious decision to eavesdrop on yourself. Seriously, you have to learn to listen to those voices with critical but not judgmental awareness. The last thing we want to do is to pour more fuel on the fire of those limiting voices and comments. Our first priority is to get to know ourselves more, and to actually learn to listen and catch that voice that is quiet and barely perceptible. At first it can seem benign and not worth the effort—after all it is just a thought, right? No, it is not "just a thought." It is the creative process working through your personal volition.

I will be repeating this throughout: Please be gentle, kind, and compassionate with yourself.

You and your life's expression can never be separated from that inner dialogue. It is imperative to understand that your thinking is a product of your consciousness. Focusing on your self-talk must be a priority because no matter what you learn and how much you read, it is all about how it lands inside of you and what you subscribe to. If you choose to believe that your self-talk is a co-creative process—and I assure you, it is—then hopefully you will prioritize listening to yourself with great curiosity through your critical thinking.

Not all self-talk is negative, of course. Your job is to learn how to discriminate and choose what to focus on. While you are learning to listen, please also commit to being kind, compassionate, and generous to yourself. It is possible that you are relearning a habit that is decades old. Let's go slow and take one step at a time so you don't get discouraged or find yourself overwhelmed. It might sound a bit dramatic, but my experience with hundreds of students over the years has taught me to slow down the pace because you could potentially be left feeling inadequate, and nothing is less true or more damaging.

The beginning of this new habit requires focus, and a stick-to-itiveness to support the reality that you are responsible for hosting the inner dialogue that creates the life you are living. This can cause some individuals to want to stop the journey immediately. Don't. Don't stop. Stay with me! I promise you that after the shock of the coming realizations settle, you will find a bounty of personal power that you might not have known was there—because it was hidden within the chaos of the "monkey mind," as Buddhists often refer to it.

To return to your authentic self, you must be able to unpack the parts gently, look at them with love and kindness, and then slowly take on new thinking habits. Whether you realize it or not your inner voice becomes your authority, the authority that you haven't before taken time to question. The reason for questioning all this thinking activity is very clear though. So much of what you think of as yours—as your thoughts—are not. You have unconsciously adopted thoughts, opinions, criticisms, and tendencies from a wider range of influences. These influences are obvious and have been emphasized in other places in this book, but let's lay them out here because of how they influence this focus.

The way we talk to our children becomes their inner voice.

—PEGGY O'MARA

As we look at this first path to authenticity, I feel compelled to speak to the importance of those of us who are parents, grandparents, caretakers, and teachers at all levels as we take a moment to reflect on the quote above: The way we talk to the children in our lives becomes their inner voice. Enough cannot be said about getting conscious and how our inner voice becomes our outer voice, and when our outer voice is spoken in earshot of anyone under our influence. The danger of being unconscious applies equally to how you adopted what you heard as your own voice and how you spoke aloud to yourself and to others.

To be of a better influence on those under your care, consider trying the fine art of intimation. Intimation happens when you speak about someone within earshot of them but not directly to them. Like knowing that your child is in the next room listening, and you turn to your spouse or partner and say, "Yeah, Terri is so creative, I can't wait to see what she makes out of herself as an adult with all that talent." What this does is it allows Terri or whoever you are speaking about to be influenced by your love and acceptance. Intimation is a great way to support anyone without trying too hard.

It's almost like taking a placebo—and for every placebo, there's also a nocebo. So, use this technique wisely.

Imagine if you had grown up hearing only wonderful things about yourself from the people around you. Just think how differently you might see yourself now.

And if you are a parent or caretaker, take this to heart: Speak with care. If you speak in a way that denigrates someone within earshot, the same effect takes hold—but in the negative. Words have power, whether whispered or shouted. Words are the seeds planted to create a new reality—plant the right seeds, the affirming seeds.

Because we influence others, especially in the role of parent or as any kind of direct and consistent caretaker, we must raise our level of awareness to the influence we have on others—most specifically our children. Children hear what we say to them and take it as authority, but they also listen to how we speak about them, and how we speak about ourselves. Please, as you read this, don't slip into any kind of feelings of guilt or shame. These concepts are not obvious to the untrained individual, and we were doing the best we could. What matters is NOW, this moment, in this new and more expansive way of looking at ourselves.

Self-talk has two components, both obvious: our inner and our outer voice. Both of these voices require a different discipline and a commitment to developing better habits, which when I say it like this can sound so clinical. But what if your new habit had everything to do with you being devoted to being kind to yourself, to being a source of love and acceptance?

Imagine a room full of people. A mother comes in carrying her newborn, and everyone gathers around to welcome this brand-new baby. As you speak words of affirmation to this baby, you might say something like this: *You are so beautiful. I am so happy you are here in this life, and my wish, want, hope, and dream for you is that you live the life of your heart's desire in every way possible. I wish for you joy, love, happiness, adventure, health, and grand prosperity.*

I could almost guarantee that you would not judge, criticize, or condemn this precious new being. You certainly wouldn't criticize it for not walking yet, not talking; that would never cross your mind. Now imagine you are that baby being held and introduced to the room of onlookers and answer this question honestly: **When did you stop deserving to hear these kind of messages?** When did you start entertaining thoughts to the contrary? You deserve to have your inner voice and your spoken voice to be in concert with each other, speaking your deserved reality into being.

If you are a parent, the same questions about your children apply. When did your children stop deserving to hear messages of love and acceptance? When did you get distracted from your children's perfection? Was it when they learned the word *no* or began to form opinions, or when they started to become the individuals they were born to be? You and your opinions go into creating your children's reality until they become spiritually emancipated and learn to think and choose for themselves.

As a loving and devoted parent who has likely made some mistakes, you can take some inventory of your parenting skills but please be gentle with yourself. (I know I have said this before, but gentleness is so necessary along this journey.) Don't use this to add to that self-limiting inner voice. Recognize that you did the best you could with the information and the consciousness you had at that time.

Your inner voice will follow your lead. Lead it toward self-acceptance and self-love. Parent yourself in a kind and loving way. Be your best cheerleader.

OUR HUMAN ADDICTIONS

There are a couple of human tendencies most of us share. I would say all of us, but that can't be true, so for the sake of this discussion I will say most. **These two specific tendencies are our addictions to being liked and to being nice.** It is important that you take time to consider these addictions at this point in our conversation. These addictions inform our authenticity, because they live at the very heart of why we often find ourselves not only inauthentic but a mere shadow of our truest essence. Because they are so globally normal, these addictions are not easy to beat or identify without making an exerted effort.

Let's begin with our deeply rooted addiction to being liked—it often begins in early childhood. Even as toddlers, we seek approval from our parents, grandparents, and other caregivers, constantly scanning their faces for clues of delight or disapproval. That longing for affirmation becomes ingrained early, shaping how we behave and who we believe we need to be to feel safe and loved.

This early conditioning is only further reinforced when we enter the school system. Any parent knows the harsh reality: Children are often exposed to unkindness, exclusion, and even cruelty in their peer environments. The emotional trauma that many children experience in school is increasingly being recognized as an epidemic—one that psychologists are now speaking about more openly, despite decades of silence in conversations about child development. In an effort to counterbalance the wounds and teach a more heart-centered way of being, many schools have begun implementing programs to promote kindness, empathy, and compassion.

But take children out of that unnatural setting. Get them engaged in life, give them responsibilities to care for something other than themselves, such as a pet or plants, or involve them in maintaining the home. Natural characteristics develop that help to create self-confidence and self-love, and their need for outside approval gives way to self-confidence and self-satisfaction, needing less from the outside.

Most children, however, are not raised at home under the careful eyes of their parents or in a small-school setting that promotes self-empowerment, schools like Montessori and other similar schools. I watched this wonderful phenomenon happen when my boys were young as we enrolled them in an amazing alternative school called The Sprout House, founded by the brilliant Joanne Lockwood White, an inspired educator. In that setting, children were encouraged to be fully involved in the earth, in forests, in activities where they measured out the flour, prepared homemade pasta, helped to cook it, and then served one another. In caring for each other, these children developed a stunning natural empathy, and none of them had time to wonder if anyone liked them.

One of my sons learned to read very late, through the school's encouragement. I trusted the process and kept him enrolled in the school. During the years he was in attendance, he wasn't reading on his own, so they had his fellow students and friends take turns reading to him. My concern was obvious: How will he see himself? Will he judge himself, feel embarrassed, or be ashamed? Much to my surprise, he began to read. He felt cared for and not judged, and the children who supported him appeared to have no opinions about it. When we finally switched him to a public school, he managed to carry with him a sense of self-confidence and no concern about being liked. Thankfully, I trusted the process.

My son's story is the exception, not the rule—unfortunately. As a spiritual coach and counselor, I have heard the exorbitant stories shared by clients and students who revealed just how much they do not feel liked, loved, or accepted.

Now the question is: What happens when we don't feel liked? We alter our way of being, we twist and turn, deny, and force ourselves into so many false versions of ourselves. We alter our behavior, our looks, how we engage others. We hide aspects of ourselves, tell lies—lots of lies—and hope in the end we will be liked and accepted for the version we created of ourselves.

The contrived version of ourselves leads to an unfortunate reality: We attract others who are also hiding behind their own manipulated personas. We end up creating relationships based on these false facades—mask to mask, wound to wound. But there's a limit to how long this can last, because as our wounds clash with the wounds of another, all hell breaks loose. The most common thing is that we project our wounds, which are our shadow aspects, onto people around us. We often believe that the other people are the problem, leaving us powerless to shift this experience, because we can't change anything that is outside of us.

Eventually, the facade crumbles, and we're left utterly exhausted from the energy spent maintaining this false bravado. As it begins to fall apart, we start to question what's wrong with us, seeking help from professionals and sometimes turning to pharmaceutical solutions that don't quite work. When these constant attempts to fix our false selves fail, depression can settle in, leaving us still wondering, "What's wrong with me?"

In extreme cases, those who need to be liked who have financial resources might even go to the extreme and have their face or body altered to the current acceptable social standard. Think Botox. And there are some who will attempt to numb the intense feelings of not-enoughness by turning to mind-altering substances. The extent that people go to is very determined by how much emotional pain they are in. Those who have financial means might turn to the current designer drug or cosmetic surgeon. Our prisons are overloaded with individuals who never got to know their authentic essence, so they leaned on desperate and unlawful ways of being. If only this pattern could have been interrupted before it got that far.

Let me say this simply: When you do not like yourself, you might attempt to become what you are not, to try and find that acceptance. I call it an addiction because it is a compelling behavior, and it is sad to witness. Some of this behavior does begin in the home—of course, and why not? If the individuals raising you are not emotionally healthy and haven't learned to love and accept themselves, how could they possibly rear children who do?

You were seduced into a way of being by your family because they wanted you to be part of your family tribe. This influence by your caretakers happens through an unconscious yet systematic set of approvals and criticisms. If you have ever heard someone being accused of having a look that could kill, that look was an attempt to silently domesticate you, a fearful one, but an attempt to domesticate. Parents who withhold affection because their child didn't get the right grades or make it onto the basketball team are domesticating them unconsciously. This can all sound ridiculous as you read it, but there is a part of you that recognizes this unfortunate phenomenon as real.

What did you do to secure family approval? Did you withhold the truth, smile when you didn't want to, kiss your uncle because you were expected to even though you know he's a creep? As children we are often forced to tolerate certain conditions because we have a need to be within our family unity. This is a common, albeit painful reality, but it's based on our need to survive.

Now, let's imagine what life can be if you could simply stop wanting or needing approval from anyone—*ever*. Imagine you being you, as you are, without seeking anyone's approval. For those of us—and I am very much one of these people—who created a false version of ourselves, as we begin to heal our inner landscape and turn our attention away from outside approval to self-acceptance and self-love, the world changes, opens up, and becomes a playground for our authentic self to play in.

It is time, dear heart, to find your way back to *you*—the authentic you that lives at the very center of your being. The you who was present at the beginning, who birthed this life with purpose and light. It is time to remember who you truly are.

Our other addiction is a bit more complicated to identify because it can be hidden so easily in socially acceptable behavior. It is our addiction to being nice. Whenever I say this, I have to follow up that statement by adding, "Of course you want to be nice," but we must establish the distinction between being nice from our insecurities and being nice from our consciousness. Identifying this distinction is worthy of your time and attention. Being nice is so expected that to question it can seem ludicrous.

You heard your mother, grandmother, and maybe your father say it over and over again: "Just be nice." Being nice seemed like a good thing, and it is what your parents were also taught. But as you, the reader, might have experienced, sometimes this simple and straightforward instruction didn't make sense at the time because you were being instructed to be nice to someone who was unkind or downright abusive. Teaching your child to be nice might seem like a solid parental thing to do, but for many people, this author included, **being nice often means ignoring what is going on behind the scenes.**

Not everybody had to deal with extreme unkind and abusive experiences, but even in a benign setting, constantly instructing a child to be kind can leave them not valuing what their feeling experience is. Not all people deserve your kindness or your niceness. It is important to learn to honor your intuition when it comes to engaging with others.

How different it would have been if your parents had instructed you to trust yourself, be honest about what you want, not to hug or kiss anyone that you are not comfortable with, and so on. What if you had been taught to show social respect toward those who earned it but to avoid contact with those who didn't make you feel safe? What a different life it could have been if we had been taught to trust ourselves and be who we are.

Of course there is a case for the parents of small children to guide them in the direction of respecting others around them. We can't necessarily expect them to have that wherewithal; that is our job as parents.

I thoroughly enjoy the performer Pink, and how she is dedicated to being herself without excuses, and she parents her daughter that way. Wow, imagine having that influence early.

My third son was a PK—a preacher's kid, and therefore subject to greater scrutiny and expectations. He grew up around a lot of wonderful and loving people. He matured quite early and was a wonderful child, but people wanted his attention so much in terms of hugs and such, I often instructed him to only hug when he wanted to. And I would run interference for him, because I did not want expectations imposed upon him. If your child does not want to approach someone, hug someone, or kiss someone, please trust them. Let them grow from their own comfort and not because they are expected to make an adult feel better.

As you continue to practice paying attention to your mind and listening to your self-talk, be on the lookout for the allure of being liked and being nice. Free yourself, my friend; you deserve it.

POWER PRACTICES FOR SELF-TALK

With each path you explore, I'll be offering practices to support your journey—because when you're seeking real change, your decisions need action behind them in order to come to fruition. Be willing to do the work. Make the shifts. And trust that *all good will follow.* Keep it playful.

These practices are simple by design. Their purpose is to raise your awareness of how you think and speak *to* and *about* yourself. Never underestimate the power of personal awareness; it's one of the most potent tools for growing into your most authentic expression.

Please have a journal dedicated to this journey, leave it at your bedside. Begin to pay attention to the first and last thoughts you have in your day and jot down a few notes to raise your awareness. *Try to do this first thing in the morning even if you need to set your alarm and wake up early for this purpose.*

- Every time you receive a phone call, use that moment just before you pick up to pause what you were thinking about as you take a breath.
- Passing by a mirror? Look into the mirror and pay attention to your thoughts. Do you look away or do you look with approval?
- When someone pays you a compliment, do you deflect it or are you gracious and receive it with a thank-you? Begin to receive compliments gracefully.
- When sharing good news with someone, do you downplay your accomplishment? Practice sharing your good news with pride yet not in a boastful way.
- Use your phone to set periodic reminders throughout the day to pause and check in with your thoughts. This can help you become more aware of your self-talk in different situations. (This is a great way to learn to understand your emotional reactions, too.)
- Spend a few minutes each day practicing mindfulness meditation. Focus on your breath and observe your thoughts without judgment. This practice can help you become more aware of your self-talk patterns.
- When you find yourself in a stressful situation, make a mental note of your thoughts. If you have the opportunity, take a moment to write down your thoughts. This can help you identify negative self-talk, so you can work on reframing it. You want to catch the thought that was sparked by the stressful moment.
- Start your day with positive affirmations. Write down a few positive statements about yourself and repeat them daily. This can help shift your self-talk to a more positive tone. (I have provided some affirmations at the end of each chapter.)

- Set your intention to speak kindly and generously to yourself and about yourself.
- Stop saying "I'm sorry" all the time. Replace it with saying, "Thank you for being patient." Being sorry all the time makes us feel pathetic.
- Stop throwing yourself under the bus when you make a mistake. Take responsibility and simply speak to the solution.
- Take compliments by just saying, "Thank you."

DANCE WITH ME IN YOUR IMAGINATION

Imagine with me a world where all people begin to cultivate kind, affirming, loving, and supportive self-talk. Imagine the energetic shift that would happen if we were devoted to being as kind to ourselves as we are to others. Imagine how gentle things would feel. Imagine how the interactions would change between individuals who loved themselves. Imagine a world in which you can trust yourself to be your own champion.

JOURNAL PROMPTS

Sit in a quiet spot, in a place that feels safe and comfortable, perhaps where you are surrounded by nature or in a room that you love. Sit in quiet stillness for a while—at least ten minutes with no phone, music, or any other distractions—and put pen to paper without thinking too much about it. Just write about whatever comes to mind. If you really want to benefit from this practice, do this daily first thing in the morning, even if you have to wake up early to do so. NO editing or critiquing what you write, just write.

* Every night before bed, make a list of the things you found yourself doing right today. What worked, what kindness, what support did you offer today?
* Did you handle a challenge well? List anything, anything that you did that felt good. If it is only one thing, so be it. Start with where you are. Then in the morning, read that list. Do this every day for at least three weeks but longer if you find your mind is still stuck on limiting ways.
* What inner language am I willing to give up for my mind to be kinder?

A SPIRITUAL MINDSHIFT TO UPLEVEL YOUR SELF-TALK

There is an open, beautiful, and loving energy that is constantly seeking to create out of itself. I know that as I open to it, I become a willing vessel through which it creates. This glorious power expresses in, through, and as me to the degree that I open to it, accept it, and invite it into my soul and my reality.

This is a stunning truth: As I surrender, I become more of it. As I open, accept, and allow it, my divine relationship with this power deepens, empowering me to access my inner intelligence and infinite resources. Through this alignment, I step into the fully expressed version of myself.

I am willing to be me—like never before—the full, undefended version of myself. I make no excuses for who I am, for my opinions, or for my expression. I show up as I was born to be—brilliant, vibrant, and wonderfully alive. I was incarnated into this life, ordained to be a force for good, a vessel through which good can be created, and a channel for wisdom and intuition. All aspects of my life and every role I play are infused with the divine energy that gave me life from the beginning.

This is my divine birthright, and so I release any and all habits of self-doubt, fear, confusion, or self-deprecating internal conversations. I release both the conscious and unconscious limitations I have adopted that have held me captive.

This leaves me standing on the mountaintop—free, unencumbered by limitations, and open to the movement of mind and heart that reveals the glory of the Divine as me.

I know that the glorious essence of this universe gives life to the spoken word, and I accept this truth fully. With a heart overflowing with gratitude, I release this word into love, into life, and into the awe of the infinite. And so it is.

A LOVE LETTER TO MYSELF

Dearest Self,

Today, I pause to express my deepest gratitude and admiration for the beautiful journey we have begun. The transformation of our inner voice—from critical and harsh to loving and supportive—has been nothing short of miraculous. I am profoundly proud of how far we've come.

There were times when you felt buried beneath negative thoughts, self-doubt, and judgment. And still—you chose to rise. You acknowledged the power within you to shift the story, to rewrite the narrative. With courage and grace, you embraced mindfulness and self-awareness, taking time each day to pause, reflect, and reframe. In doing so, you've created a sanctuary of kindness and love within your own mind.

I see your commitment to those gentle check-ins throughout the day. Those little reminders to observe your thoughts—they matter. They've become a sacred practice, anchoring you in awareness and allowing you to lovingly redirect your self-talk when needed. I am grateful for your willingness to notice patterns, to write things down, to see what no longer serves you, and to choose a new possibility.

Your dedication to shift habits has been a gift—a nurturing balm. By coming back to the breath and witnessing your thoughts without judgment, you've cultivated a relationship with yourself that is compassionate, steady, and real. It's changed everything.

The way you begin your mornings—with affirmations that soothe your heart—has created a powerful shift. You've set a new tone. You've taught your inner voice to be your cheerleader, your comfort, your truth-teller.

You've sat in stillness, allowed your thoughts to flow, and listened. You've honored your growth, celebrated your kindness, and witnessed your evolution. Because of your consistent, loving effort, a new voice lives within you now. One that uplifts. One that encourages. One that never forgets your inherent worth.

I celebrate you, dear Self, for all that you've done to get here. May your loving inner voice continue to guide you, nurture you, and reflect back the radiant truth of who you are.

With all my love and appreciation,
Me

REMEMBER TO BREATHE

Remember that breath is a gift of the beloved. Begin to use your breath to raise your body awareness. Use your breath as the focal point throughout your day. This practice will help you to build your mindfulness and body awareness, two good things to grow on.

Let's Conclude with These Affirmations

- ✶ I now give myself permission to speak my world into beautiful form.
- ✶ I choose words that affirm my truth, my beauty, and my becoming.
- ✶ I speak only words of self-love and acceptance, as I shine.
- ✶ **I demand to be me—without excuses.**

PEARLS OF WISDOM

Your inner voice is the most important influence you have, and it never shuts off. The first thing to do when you are seeking to retrieve your personal power and authenticity is to learn how to listen to and monitor that inner voice, and then match your outer voice with your inner voice. Since you can never be outside or away from it, the most important thing for you to do is to learn how to make that voice a friendly, conducive, self-empowering, loving voice. When you get a handle on this inner voice and your outer words and you sync them up, you will begin to immediately move your life to an experience of great joy and beauty. Start today.

2

SEE YOURSELF WITH BRAVE AND HONEST EYES

The Dance with Self-Awareness

You may not control all the events that happen to you, but you can decide not to be reduced by them.

—MAYA ANGELOU

Description of Self-Awareness

Self-awareness is the practice of looking within to understand all that motivates your thoughts, emotions, and actions to the degree that you are able to understand yourself and love yourself unconditionally and with compassion.

Here Is a Quick Start Option

Beginning today, pay attention to your thinking, behavior, and tendencies. Pay close attention to any knee-jerk reactions, and when you are in reaction, ask yourself what it is about.

Self-awareness is one of the most important aspects of personal emancipation and empowerment while being one of the most underappreciated. Some of the advantages of self-awareness are improved emotional regulation, such as in having a calm and settled body, being a better decision-maker for all your life's precious moments, and experiencing greatly improved relationships. You see, once you know who you are and what moves you, you can then make fitting decisions and choose who you want to be with as you attract new friendships and love relationships from your authentic self and not from your conditioned self.

Getting to know yourself with the intent to grow your awareness is not a complicated process but it is a high, holy, and sacred experience. I label it high, holy, and sacred because your journey here is all about emancipating your small human self, with a small *s*, to your higher SELF, with all caps, which is the self of you that connects with the universal self, as we mentioned earlier in the book.

When I was a young pup, I thought that being aware meant that I had to be aware of everything that was going on everywhere around me all the time. Could you imagine if that were true—that would be totally crazy-making. Clearly, I had the wrong idea. I recently turned to my Facebook family and asked people to describe what they thought self-awareness was. The answers were many and varied, and wonderful to read. The description I offered above was an aggregate of those answers.

Getting to know youself is like writing a love letter to your inner being, offering your full attention to the parts of you that are seeking love and acknowledgment. From a very young age, most children crave attention, as they call to their parents throughout the day, "Watch me, Mom," "Watch me, Dad," or even "Watch me, Nana." To a child, your loving attention means everything. It tells them, "I see you, and I love you."

Cultivating self-awareness is a declaration to look deeply at yourself—without turning away, without judgment, and without feeling the need to change anything. The you that you've always been holds within the movement, power, and resources that may not yet have names. As your self-awareness grows, you may discover more and more reasons to love and accept yourself and to celebrate the Presence of the Divine expressing Itself through you.

In my twenties, after having my first child, I walked through life in a body that the outer world seemed to find attractive. But at the time, I was unaware of this fact—at least not to the degree reflected by the attention I received. When I entered a room or a restaurant and noticed someone looking at me, my first thought wasn't *Oh, they find me attractive.* Instead, my instinctive, unconscious reaction was *What's wrong with me? Why are they staring?* Instead of relishing the attention, I judged myself, feeling completely self-conscious and afraid. That tendency to be self-conscious would stay with me for years. Painful but true.

The sad truth for many women—not all, but many—is that we often seek attention as a form of approval. Some are fully aware of their attractiveness, while others move gingerly through life, uncertain of what's going on, missing the opportunity to enjoy the attention. There's something both amusing and bittersweet about aging. We become acutely aware of how much we didn't appreciate what we had—whether it was our beauty, the power that beauty could wield, or the doors it could open. We often lacked the awareness to appreciate what we had until we lost it.

Now, as an older woman, I look back at my journey with great amusement. Thankfully, I do not live in regret over missed moments, but this is possible only because I've learned to embrace and love my authentic self. My self-love grows in proportion to my self-awareness.

There is a version of you that has been dulled by human tendencies and everyday distractions. But as you begin to apply the suggestions I offer—alongside the journal prompts and spiritual mindshifts—an unexpected treasure will begin to reveal itself—YOU—untamed and unguarded.

The clearest example I can offer from my own life is this: Now, in my sixties, I find myself an author. That only became possible when I began to trust the intelligence within me and felt worthy of letting it be expressed and shared. I didn't seek out a publisher; I was invited. When we change our mind and put energy behind it, it miraculously happens.

This is what happens when we stop trying to force life into what we *think* it should be—and instead open to acceptance and allowance.

When you finally remove the mask that has kept you captive, the most beautiful version of yourself will and must be revealed. I say it must be revealed because this is your divine birthright.

As a teacher of forgiveness and shadow work, I am honored to witness students grow their self-awareness through these healing practices. My students, as they begin to learn about their internal and emotional motivation born of many things, including their child-rearing and trauma, quickly find their awareness to be curative. Awareness combined with wise choices redirects one to a more authentic and glorious life.

Growing self-awareness can conjure up a new world of possibilities, a life of freedom. When you know what causes you to move toward or away from someone, instead of being on automatic, you will learn about your internal conditioning and that is a necessary feature in order to redirect your attention.

RAISING YOUR FEELING AWARENESS

One powerful practice I often use with my coaching clients is a method for tuning in to your emotions throughout the day. It's simple, accessible, and incredibly eye-opening. All you need is a watch or your phone with an alarm, something most of us have on hand.

Here's how it works: For at least one week, set an alarm on your phone to go off at regular intervals. This could be every hour, every two hours, or every three hours, depending on what feels manageable for you. Each time the alarm sounds, pause and ask yourself this simple yet profound question: What am I feeling right now?

Take a moment to really tune in. Avoid overanalyzing or trying to justify your emotions. Instead, focus on labeling them—whether it's joy, anxiety, contentment, frustration, or even neutrality. Then, jot down your response in a small journal or a notes app you can keep handy.

This practice does two things. First, it helps you develop a habit of checking in with yourself, which is crucial for cultivating self-awareness. Second, it creates a record of your emotional patterns over time. You might notice that certain feelings arise more frequently during specific parts of your day or in response to particular circumstances.

As you track your emotions, remember to approach yourself with compassion. There's no "wrong" way to feel. This exercise isn't about fixing anything; it's about understanding yourself on a deeper level. By the end of the first week, you'll have a greater sense of your inner landscape and a clearer understanding of the ebb and flow of your emotional world.

Give yourself permission to be curious, open, and nonjudgmental. You may be surprised at how much you learn. As always, be gentle with yourself. You are a stunning work in progress.

RAISING YOUR THINKING AWARENESS

This practice is not for the faint of heart—it is for those who are ready to take an honest, compassionate look at what's really rolling around inside your mind. The answers that arise from this exercise are often deep, meaningful, and illuminating. However, they absolutely *must* be received without judgment. This practice isn't about critiquing yourself; it's about observing, understanding, and ultimately freeing yourself from the unconscious filters that shape your perceptions.

Judgments are a powerful indicator of what you believe about yourself and thc world around you. While many of your judgments may appear to be about others, they are always a reflection of your inner world—of your beliefs, fears, and even what intimidates or challenges you. This can be a humbling realization, as many of my students are initially surprised to discover just how frequently they judge, especially if they believed themselves to be nonjudgmental.

The process may occasionally disrupt your peace, as seeing your mind clearly can be uncomfortable. But discomfort is often the first step toward transformation. Please be gentle with yourself. (I know, I know, I have said it again.) This exercise is not about labeling yourself as "bad" or "wrong"; it is a tool for growing your self-awareness, not a weapon for self-criticism.

Begin by observing your thoughts throughout the day, particularly moments when you notice yourself forming judgments.

Ask yourself:

* *What am I thinking right now?*
* *What belief might be fueling this judgment?*
* *How does this judgment reflect something I feel about myself or the world?*

Write your observations down without censoring or overthinking. Over time, patterns may emerge that reveal what's truly blocking the revelation of your authenticity. The more aware you become of how your mind operates, the more freedom you'll have to choose love, acceptance, and understanding—both for yourself and others. This awareness is the first step to living in alignment with your true, authentic self.

Learn to Love Yourself

While this book concludes with a chapter on self-love, the journey truly begins with awareness, as you discover who you are, what motivates you, and how much goodness already resides within you. Self-love doesn't happen at once, it is cultivated, moment by moment, through small, intentional acts of kindness toward yourself. So, let's eat dessert first—you know, in case you don't get to the last chapter.

RAISING YOUR BODY AWARENESS

You are not just your thoughts; you are consciousness expressing itself through your body temple. It is critically important to learn how to read the messages your body is constantly sending you.

When we spend so much of our lives reacting and responding to external stimulation, we develop ingrained reactions. Over time, we may start experiencing physical responses without even catching the thoughts behind them.

There are two essential things to understand here:

Uninterrupted, your thoughts will create physical reactions, which, if left unchecked, can lead to illness and disease in the extreme, or at the least lead to anxiety, stress, and depression.

When you learn to pay attention, name your emotions, and understand their origins, you gain valuable self-knowledge, uncover areas that need healing, and prevent these sensations from becoming part of your shadow.

Your body is a barometer, and the more you learn to read it, the more you can grow from the sensations you identify.

Just as I have instructed you to watch your thoughts, you can apply the same practice to cultivate your body awareness. One simple way is to set an alarm periodically throughout the day and, when it goes off, pause and check in with your body. Notice what sensations arise.

But there is an even more profound practice.

Try this:

1. Sit in a comfortable, meditative position.
2. Close your eyes and begin a slow, deliberate body scan, moving from the top of your head to the tips of your toes.
3. Pay close attention to every sensation—without trying to fix or adjust anything. Simply observe and take note.
4. If you encounter areas of stress or discomfort, breathe into those places and direct your full attention there.
5. Silently ask each part of your body: What do you need me to know?

By practicing this regularly, you will develop a deep and intuitive connection with your physical self, transforming your body from something you simply inhabit into a trusted guide for healing and self-awareness.

This is another exercise that is much lighter than some of the deeper practices you may have encountered, but don't let its simplicity fool you. It is a powerful tool for shifting your focus from self-criticism to self-appreciation. Every night, before you go to bed, grab your journal and make a list of all the things you did right that day. (If you began this exercise already, good for you. It can be used to grow so many wonderful things inside of you.) Reflect on the small wins, the acts of kindness, the moments of courage, and even the times you simply showed up when it would have been easier not to.

Let your list include everything you can think of, no matter how small it might seem:

* Did you listen deeply to a friend? Write it down.
* Did you give yourself a moment of rest when you needed it? That counts, too.
* Did you smile at a stranger, finish a task, or take a step toward a personal goal?

Celebrate it. All of it. Because all of it matters, and all of it is you.

The purpose of this exercise is to gently retrain your mind to notice and acknowledge your goodness. Over time, you'll start to see yourself through a kinder lens, recognizing the beauty, generosity, and positive impact you bring to the world. If you struggle at first to find things to appreciate about yourself, that's okay. Start small and trust that with practice, the process will become easier.

The more you consciously track your moments of "rightness," the more they will grow, and the more you'll begin to truly *see* yourself as the remarkable person you already are.

Learning to love yourself is not about perfection, it's about embracing who you are, moment by moment, with tenderness and gratitude. Let this simple practice be the foundation upon which your ultimate journey of self-love and authenticity continues to flourish.

Always remember the goal with these spiritual practices are to move you to a greater self-love. If your internal dialogue begins to go haywire, stop what you're doing, slow down, and reset your intention to be one of exploring and expanding your self-awareness in order to experience the fullness of you. It is all right there within you; your job is to remove the veil that is keeping you blind.

Please also keep in mind that what you are looking *for* and what you are looking *with* are the same. You have an entire inner landscape of creativity, strength, and genius that has been tamped down by the conditioning of the planet—all in a very unconscious way. These practices are part of how you will open and walk along the portal that leads you to YOU, your glorious, beautiful essence. If, when you read these words, your doubt comes up, face that doubt, look at it directly and declare, "I am so much more than this. I am the evidence of this glorious, loving intelligence."

I want to share with you that I really, really, really needed this practice and I wish someone had guided me much earlier in my life to this particular practice, because I wasted years feeling doubtful about myself. Now I say, "Screw that; I am worthy of an extraordinary life and know this is the path to get there."

LIVING AN UNDEFENDED LIFE

TO LIVE AN UNDEFENDED LIFE IS TO LIVE THE LIFE THAT YOU WERE ORDAINED TO LIVE—AT BIRTH, AT THE TIME OF CONCEPTION, UNTAINTED, UNTAMED, AND UNCONDITIONED BY HUMAN INFLUENCES.

Hard to imagine, isn't it? What does this even mean? It is an invitation to live a life without explaining yourself or making excuses.

How do we even go about living this way? Well, as Albert Einstein is credited with saying: "We cannot solve our problems with the same thinking we used when we created them." So, jump into these pages with unbridled curiosity and wonder, leave your automatic thinking behind. Grow the new habit of conscious uncertainty, which means letting go of what you think you know so you can uncover the infinite expressions that life has to offer.

You must find a way to break free from your usual and consistent ways of being. You must entertain new ideas, ask questions, fanning the fires of curiosity and breaking down the walls of normal. You must learn to be uncomfortable and draw outside the lines while taking risks and doing so without a safety net. And you must do this because you will be rewarded with a new, fully expressed you.

> As Guillaume Apollinaire wrote, "'Come to the edge,' he said. 'We can't, we're afraid!' they responded. 'Come to the edge,' he said. 'We can't, we will fall!' they responded. 'Come to the edge,' he said. And so they came. And he pushed them. And they flew."

You will fly because it is your divine birthright to fly—trust the unfolding process but do so courageously.

This is a great time to talk about two practices that might seem unnatural at first. These practices are to (1) question everything and (2) doubt your certainty about what you think is true. Yes, I said *doubt* because there is a vast wealth of newness behind the parts of you that you will be questioning. If you are always certain, there will be no room for growth and expansion. A certain mind can be a confident mind but a mind that is always certain is not open to what it does not know.

To doubt what you think is true will open up new avenues of creativity so you can find out who you really are. As you move through this book, you will be looking at the many paths of the self to free you from what is. When you are willing to be uncertain, you are saying to the Creative Source of this glorious universe: Show me; show me what I don't know. It takes one who is willing to be humble and to surrender certainty to make room for the new and the unknown.

Of course, there is a level of self-doubt that is counterproductive, but let's be clear here in this distinction. I am not suggesting that you entertain the kind of self-doubt that tears at your confidence. I am suggesting that you release the habits of being so sure you know what is true that you never open the next door of discovery. You must free your thinking.

There is a silly story told to emphasize the lack of questioning things and not being logical.

One holiday, a husband walks into the kitchen as his wife is preparing the holiday ham. He watches as she cuts off both ends of the ham, as she has done so many times before. But curious, the husband asks, "Hon, why do you cut off the ends of the ham?" The wife answers, "I don't know; go ask my mother," and so he did. He walked upstairs to the third-floor apartment, knocked, walked in, and asked his mother-in-law, "Why do you cut off both ends of the ham when you cook the holiday ham?" She answered him saying, "I don't know; go ask Grandma," and so he did. Now he walked down to the first-floor apartment and knocked at the door. When she opened the door, he asked the same question: "Grandma, why do you cut off both ends of the ham for the holiday ham?" She said, "I don't, unless I can't get it into the pan."

You see, the next two generations of women didn't question, didn't doubt the logic of what and why they were doing something. They simply rinsed and repeated what they saw. Without a commitment to questioning and doubting, without curiosity, we live the life that our parents lived, and our grandparents did, and so on and so forth.

To break free from the unspoken but very strong conditioning of family and the tribes you belong to, to live an undefended life, you must begin by knowing what that conditioning is.

Carolyn Myss, in her seminal book, *Anatomy of the Spirit*, taught so clearly about our need to be part of a tribe. A tribe indicates a unit of a particular culture. You can be part of many tribes simultaneously. As a woman, women are my tribe. Being of Irish blood, the Irish is another cultural tribe. With my spiritual practices and claiming to be a metaphysician places me in another tribe. Tribes can keep you feeling safe; but depending upon the strength and conditions of the tribe, you might feel more like you are being held captive.

I learned a lot about humans and our tendencies with this new distinction. I came to understand why certain people were so attached to their family traditions. To break those traditions meant they were going to risk being cast out or at least criticized. This is just another way of looking at our domestication.

There are spiritual, religious, and many Indigenous cultures from around the world, some of which have very strong rules and expectations about what it takes to be in that particular tribe, and questioning the rules or testing them can leave you shunned and forced to live on your own and never allowed back in. This way of being is quite severe and, to this day, it remains quite common.

Some people need to remain within the confines of the culture they were raised in, and some want nothing to do with it and choose to break free. Who are YOU? Do you choose to live within or without the tribe that you were reared in?

To live an undefended life, one must be willing to take the risk of their individuality. When you were a child and climbing a tree, you would sometimes be tempted to climb out on the skinny branches because you wanted to see more clearly, but it was risky, and you would have to decide whether the risk of climbing out there was worth the chance you were taking.

It is likely you took these risks when you were growing up. Other risks might have been delving into drinking with friends, smoking pot, or trying more serious drugs. You took risks when you wanted to hang with the cool kids, but it meant that you had to lie about where you were going, who you were hanging with, and what you were doing. You were always deciding whether or not to go for what looked like fun; was it worth getting caught and possibly getting punished? As children, we begin early to lie and hide and pretend we were something and someone that we weren't as we tried to fit in to belong to a tribe that looked better than the one we already belonged to. Can you identify memories of this behavior?

Let's look at the practice of lying and how it has impacted us. There was a time in our lives when we started to perfect the art of lying—or at least we thought so. Some of our parents knew we were lying but didn't want to create a fuss that might cause us to pull away. How many lies did you tell so you could go where you wanted, do what you wanted, and hang out with the friends that you wanted? Do you remember how easily you justified the lies?

Telling lies became a coping mechanism that, over time, we perfected.

As long as the lie existed, we were able to manage our current decisions. This is another step in creating inauthentic lives—as necessary as it might have felt. If we are following along, we can see how we began to create who we were a very long time ago. The path back to our beautiful, authentic self is paved with many paths, and we are working to unpack them and find the road signs to bring us back home to ourselves.

Because lying has many effects, I would put extra time aside to unpack this habit. Sometimes our lies seem so justified that we might not even notice it. This is an invitation to grow our awareness and retrieve some of the personal power initially lost in the illusion of false protection. This is the time for you to be YOU!

If you are wondering why I seem so focused on lying, it is because when I was young, I was an incessant liar. Yes, I had reasons when I was young. Those reasons had to do with protecting myself (or so I thought), but even after I didn't need to protect myself any longer, I continued the habit. It wasn't until I gained some self-awareness that it all changed.

Things to Ponder

(Remember to be radically honest here; it is an important component to your freedom.) Here are some questions for you to get honest with yourself as you begin this journey. When you ponder, find a quiet place to sit, have a journal with you, and just respond without thinking.

* What lies did I tell and why did I tell them?
* Did I feel the need to defend myself and my way of being; and if yes, how did I do that?
* Did I take risks, or was the fear too much for me?
* What were the consequences of my lies, both to myself and to others?
* In what situations do I find it most difficult to tell the truth?
* How do I feel emotionally after telling a lie?
* Have I lied to avoid confrontation, and how has that affected my relationships?

* What truths am I afraid to face, and why?
* What are the long-term impacts of my dishonesty on my integrity and self-respect?
* How do I justify my lies to myself, and are these justifications valid?

What do you do with all the new awarenesses you uncover? Look at them, feel into them, take time to appreciate this new growing edge. And as always, be gentle. Remember, when it comes to your motivation for lying, you lied to feel safe and to protect yourself.

Now as you journey this path back home to your fully authentic self, you will no longer need to lie. Now you can choose to be you—fully, completely.

POWER PRACTICES FOR SELF-AWARENESS

Grow your self-awareness by getting to know yourself as you dialogue with your inner self. Take a moment to imagine sitting across from your self—the version of you that is wise, calm, and deeply intuitive. Write a dialogue in which you ask your inner self the following questions, and then respond as though that part of you is speaking:

> *What do I most need to hear right now? What part of me is seeking more attention and care? What is one thing I can do to nurture my sense of wholeness?*

Try a daily getting-to-know-myself practice that is grounded in the present moment. Ask yourself these questions on a daily basis and listen deeply for the answers.

* Right now, in this moment, my body feels . . .
* If my heart could describe this moment, it would say . . .

- What I appreciate about this day so far is . . .
- If I could anchor myself in one thing that makes me feel safe, it would be . . .

Take some time to reflect upon the part of your path that you have already walked upon and appreciate what you have done so far.

- A lesson that life keeps teaching me over and over is . . .
- I can see how I've grown by the lessons I learned from my teachers, parents, caregivers, and so on, because they were a positive influence in the following ways . . .
- If I could give a gift to my future self, it would be . . .

Your awareness will expand as you take inventory of the part of your journey that you have already walked upon. It is important to give yourself credit.

Learning to track your emotions is a key practice to grow your self-awareness.

Don't be too surprised if this is challenging. In my career as a teacher and coach, I have encountered more people than you could possibly imagine who do not know how to identify what they are feeling.

DANCE WITH ME IN YOUR IMAGINATION

Imagine a world in which all people expand their self-awareness to truly understand who they are, how they impact the world, and make choices to support a loving, compassionate planet for all people. Just imagine how that would feel and show up.

JOURNAL PROMPTS

Write freely in your journal without editing or judging what you write. The freer you are with yourself, the more the wisdom will rise through you. And while I say to "write" in your journal, that could also be doodling, sketching, and writing music to express yourself. Don't hold back. Express your heart. Finish these sentences:

* When I feel truly seen and loved, it is usually because . . .
* A moment in my life when I felt deeply connected to myself was . . .
* If my inner child could speak to me today, they would say . . .
* I often feel most alive when I am . . .
* If I were to write a love letter to myself, the first line would be . . .
* The part of myself that I struggle to understand but want to know better is . . .
* The qualities I admire most in others are . . . and what that tells me about myself is . . .

LETTER TO THE INNER LANDSCAPE OF SELF

Dear Heart,

I am ready to travel together to our inner landscape. I am ready to take inventory of all our gifts, faults, influences, beliefs, fears, and anything that motivates us. I am ready to dive into the depth of our essence with the intention of understanding all that makes up who we are, why we are, and where our influences come from. I am eager to free us from the struggles and trappings of the collective influence that has found its way into our subconscious.

I am thrilled as our self-awareness opens doors to our skills, talents, and the universal intelligence that is available to all. I am confident of this because I know intellectually that we are one with the universal intelligence and love, and now I am willing to know this reality deep in my being, in the very cells of our body.

Yes, I am willing to be grown from the genius that exists. I am willing to see the parts of me that I have rejected and denied and wish now to acknowledge and accept these parts. This will become possible because I am willing to look within without reservation. I am willing to see all of my influences.

Oh, dear heart, let us journey together using a practice of self-awareness to conquer the dark and let in the light. Together we will move to an experience of spiritual authenticity.

Love,
Your Inner You

A SPIRITUAL MINDSHIFT TO UPLEVEL YOUR SELF-AWARENESS

I am surrounded by a power, a presence, and an intelligence that infiltrates my being. As I sit here, basking in the beauty of silence—both external and internal—I discover a subtle stillness that reveals who I truly am. I am ready to journey deep into the inner landscape of my being, allowing me to unfurl the feathers of my flight.

In this quiet, I am drawn to open every facet of my being—to be seen, loved, and valued. I welcome the opportunity to know the finest details that have shaped me, embracing them without judgment. I am willing to expand my self-awareness to heights that grant me wisdom, intelligence, and intuition far beyond my current understanding. In this sacred unveiling, I am revealed.

This process of self-study flows through me with power and grace. The Spirit that creates and re-creates from itself is always seeking a vessel, and as my self-awareness deepens, I become increasingly available for its expression. With a heart full of gratitude for the activity of the universal law working through me, I surrender to its infinite wisdom.

In awe of life itself, I release this word to love and to law, knowing they are fulfilled in perfect harmony. And so it is.

A LOVE LETTER TO MYSELF: THE PATH OF SELF-AWARENESS (AN EXTRA LETTER JUST BECAUSE . . .)

Dearest Self,

Today I pause to honor the sacred path I've chosen—the path of self-awareness. This journey has asked for your courage, honesty, and willingness to look within. And you've shown up, again and again.

You might have once been asleep, moving through life on autopilot, but now you have opened your eyes. You notice our patterns, question your reactions, and listen more deeply to your inner world. That is no small thing. Congratulations, you beautiful being, you.

There were moments when what you saw within felt uncomfortable or unclear, but still, you stayed. You breathed through it. You asked questions instead of rushing to answers. Your willingness to grow and witness your own becoming without judgment is something to be deeply proud of. This path isn't always easy, but it is true. And in walking it, you are learning to know yourself—not just as you've been told to be, but as you really are.

Thank you for your commitment to presence, reflection, and growth. May you continue to meet yourself with curiosity and love, step by step, breath by breath. I love you, dear heart.

With deep appreciation,
Me as my whole Self

REMEMBER TO BREATHE

Sit in a quiet place and, with each inhale, affirm, "I am ready to accept all of me," and with each exhale, affirm, "I release anything in the way."

Do this for four to five minutes with focused attention.

Let's Conclude with These Affirmations

- I give myself permission to know myself fully and completely.
- I turn inward with curiosity, courage, and reverence.
- I love and adore the me I have come to know.
- **I demand to be me—without excuses.**

PEARLS OF WISDOM

It is not an exaggeration for me to say that most people have no clue why they do what they do. I have met thousands of individuals throughout my career, and only a small portion of these individuals have taken on the task to truly understand who they are and why they do what they do. Learning about your internal motivation and learning to understand the conditioning that you have adapted is key to freeing yourself from both. Once you understand the depth of who you are, you can then begin to redirect your attention and your habits, but not before then. Any habits you have are restrictive and need to be questioned.

Growing your self-awareness is akin to further freedom and authenticity. And the wonderful thing is there's a lot about you that's worthy of love. Enjoy getting to know you, the way you were born to be.

3

ASKING THE QUESTIONS THAT WAKE YOU UP

The Dance of Self-Inquiry and Contemplation: Asking the Questions That Lead You Home

The practice of peace and reconciliation is one of the most vital and artistic of human actions.

—THICH NHAT HANH

DESCRIPTION OF SELF-INQUIRY AND CONTEMPLATION

Self-Inquiry and Contemplation is the practice of asking meaningful questions of yourself while listening deeply to your inner wisdom. Through consistent practice, it can uncover profound motivations, offering clarity on why you think, feel, and act as you do.

HERE IS A QUICK START OPTION

Every day, put a few minutes aside to sit—just sit. And while you are sitting, look around your world. In a journal, jot down what you see and how you feel about what you see. You are not looking for anything specific; you are growing your observation of the self you are.

The art of self-inquiry and contemplation is a practice that may initially feel confusing, overwhelming, or like getting lost in the maze of your own mind. However, if you stay with it, you will discover an abundance of inner resources that have been patiently waiting to be discovered. Don't confuse it with navel-gazing or self-indulgence, which is a way that we feed our ego. Instead think of it as taking time to read to yourself about yourself with an air of curiosity that can lead to awe. The awe is grounded in self-discovery, which is a beautiful thing.

It takes courage to look within and explore the infinite influences that have shaped you into who you are. But once you commit to this journey, you will come to realize that you hold not only the questions but also the answers. Through this practice, you will awaken a deeper sense of self—one that holds profound wisdom, innate beauty, and intuitive guidance, empowering you to make powerful and aligned decisions in your life.

Becoming a Practitioner

A few decades ago, I walked the path of becoming a spiritual prayer practitioner in the philosophy that I eventually became a minister in. A prayer practitioner is a licensed position in our organization and requires a couple years of study. The purpose is to use positive affirmative prayer for ourselves and others. That journey was one of the earliest stepping stones to the work I do now. The training I received was life-transforming because it taught me to embody the very qualities of life that matter most to me. And that is what I want to share with you.

While my journey began with Dr. Rita Sperling, a teacher who has since passed away, it was this additional practitioner training that allowed me to fully apply all I had learned from her but couldn't because she left this life so early. Her teachings still resonate within me today, guiding me from her transcended self. Some of our most meaningful guides and teachers live within us beyond their earthly life expression.

I found practitioner training at one of the lowest points in my life—a time of deep pain, confusion, and darkness. Sometimes your suffering can light your path to a new you. I am grateful that this training did this for me. I pulled myself up out of my dark time by applying prayer and principles. (I now refer to prayers as mindshifts.*)*

To be a practitioner, specifically a spiritual prayer practitioner, is to learn the art of listening—not just to the words spoken, but beyond them. We prayer practitioners worked with people to use positive prayer for whatever they came to us for. They told us their prayer request, and their reason for the request. Often, they came to us with very difficult experiences they were having and usually wanted to tell the whole "story" they had created around the experience. We were taught to listen to them, but not necessarily the "story" as they were telling it. The person was often lost in the details of struggle and limitation, but the practitioner's role is to see through *the clutter and chaos to what is possible, to what is waiting to emerge. We then take this listening; transform it into something healing, powerful, and freeing; and conclude with a spoken word. As we know today, as suggested by our interpretation of quantum principles, the spoken word has impact.*

Though this training was meant to serve clients, it turned out to be exactly what I needed for myself—to cut through my own self-imposed bullshit and to dismantle the limiting stories I had subscribed to for so long. Self-contemplation is my favorite spiritual principle but, married to my spoken word—the mindshift—my world becomes malleable and open to divine intervention.

Let me share how contemplation serves me. I used to be someone who had fairly strong opinions about many things in life, but I learned along my journey that I needed to be open to what I didn't know, because if I never looked beyond my own knowing, how could I expand? The habit that presented itself to me looked like this: Someone would say something that would cause a reaction in me, but instead of shutting down, I would sit and contemplate what was said to see if there was something for me to learn. This caused me to be open, coachable, and more empathic throughout my life.

Self-contemplation and the practice of inquiry became my most treasured paths to freedom. And here's what I know: There is no problem, no question, no struggle that does not have a clear, powerful, and creative solution within our inner landscape. It is all right there. Nothing to be acquired, only to be mined and examined. Everything you seek already exists within you—if you are willing to sit in stillness, dive deep, and listen to the wisdom that is inherently yours, you will be guided and empowered to shed the layers of doubt and fear and embrace a new version of you.

You are not at the mercy of what was in your life—not now, not ever—but to experience this freedom, you must first know what is there, what has been living in your inner landscape. And if your inner landscape contains some weeds and seeds of limitations, it is important for you to see them, question their authority, and then choose wisely about what to give your attention to. In other words—pluck those nasty little weeds right out of your inner landscape so they do not grow to full fruition. Only by challenging yourself to think through and past what seems real or obvious will you be able to uproot those weeds and choose differently.

Self-inquiry turns your attention from the outer world of influence to the inner landscape of empowerment. There is a treasure chest of tools waiting for you to uncover and actualize, and it is necessary to do so. The millions of individuals practicing mindfulness all around the world have trained themselves to notice and acknowledge the ebb and flow of influences as they practice stillness and listening.

Learning to be still, meditate, and listen deeply will support you in this process of inquiry. While you might be starting now, it is important to know that this is a lifetime practice. After establishing this new habit of thinking, it will be automatic because once you begin to discover the influences in your life and benefit from recognizing them, you will want to continue to look and feel and acknowledge those things that have formed the foundation of your life. And once you see what they are, you will begin to choose to have it change; you will learn that your attention has so much to do with your path. Your attention to your intention to be free is a powerful combination.

Can you remember back to your childhood when you would sometimes sit and daydream? At times, your parents or maybe your teachers would admonish you to stop your daydreaming, but what they didn't know is that they were interrupting your creative process. You were imagining your desired world on your terms. I can remember sitting in the large wingback chair in our living room, and when Dad was at work and Mom was in bed, intoxicated, I would sit there and imagine my world so different from what I was experiencing. Those times of daydreaming, which I now think of as contemplation, were my way of escaping the dark and depressing atmosphere that I lived in.

This time of contemplation and imagining created the life I live today. I currently live in a world where I am free to create, love, and flourish. As you take time to sit and inquire within, contemplate upon your desired outcomes and imagine a new becoming. Your world will respond accordingly because you have been divinely connected to the universal intelligence that makes it so, whether you realize it or not.

This is YOUR time and your life, but you must create it.

In case you are tempted to flash back to when you watched the movie *The Secret* and imagined the universe as a cosmic genie—let's get real. There is no genie, and while your thoughts and contemplations are powerful, they most often do *not* result in instant manifestation. This process, this Principle, is not a vending machine in which you insert a thought and out pops your dream.

You will need to cultivate some new habits—healthy ones.

True creation happens through a shift in consciousness. Contemplation, inquiry, and imagination are sacred tools that help you expand your awareness and align with the deeper truth of who you are. And from that space, everything in your outer world begins to reflect the transformation occurring within. You don't get what you want—you get who you are in consciousness, which, in all fairness, is not always easy to recognize.

Here is my personal philosophy: consciousness first, consciousness always. Why? Because it is through your consciousness that you ultimately create your world. The goal here is not to try to force your life into a form that reflects your dreams. The goal and intention is to cultivate the consciousness of receptivity. As we do this, we become a walking, talking vibration of faith, cultivating the conviction to demonstrate our heart's desires through our personal evolution to Love.

But for some like me, many of us were reared in households with emotionally unhealthy and unskilled parents who didn't know how to encourage awareness in children. We developed according to our parents' limited knowledge. Unwittingly, we garnered extremely limited thinking. Because it is human nature to copy the behavior that is modeled, our adopted habits were set on low productivity, often negative in nature, and in no way affirming.

I wouldn't be surprised at all if you found yourself asking questions such as these:

* *What the hell is wrong with me?*
* *Why do I always do that?*
* *Why can't I get this right?*
* *Why am I always afraid?*
* *Why do I keep making the same mistakes?*
* *Why doesn't anyone like me, see me, want to be with me?*
* *Why does everything I try turn to shit?*

On and on and on.

For some spiritual types, these questions will be dismissed because they question the value of looking at the darker side of our personality and traits. Those people want only to be positive and never want to look at the shadow side, which is called the practice of *spiritual bypass.* Spiritual bypass is the act of ignoring what *is* in the hope of demonstrating one's desires. In my book *Shadow Work: A Spiritual Path to Healing and Integration,* I drive the point home that your shadow is not dark or evil, so we do not need to ignore it or condemn it by our lack of attention. It is simply a repository for what *was*, meaning for the collection of all your rejected parts. Only love and tenderness will allow you to do this deep dive as you learn to love the whole of you without exception.

Through growing your awareness, setting your intention to be your fully expressed authentic self and investing mindful quiet time, will take you into the depths of your beautiful inner landscape. You, too, will be able to alter your life-limiting self-inquiries through life-enhancing questions. How will you know your questions are life-enhancing and expressing your authentic self? You will *physically feel* the difference. Your body will tell you because your body never lies.

When I teach workshops and classes and facilitate retreats, I always offer this kind of experience or something similar to the attendees. The purpose of this exercise is to raise awareness about how our attention and spoken word creates our feeling experience.

This is what the exercise is like (do try this at your next retreat):

> *I break the attendees into dyads (groups of two), then I instruct them to participate fully and not hold back, explaining that if they do not lean into the exercise, they will miss the experience. I instruct them to sit facing each other, close enough for their knees to touch, then . . .*
>
> *Part 1. For one to two minutes, depending on the length of the time you have, Partner A speaks aloud to their partner. I give them permission to bitch, moan, and complain incessantly and very energetically. Partner B does nothing but listen—there's no responding or talking, just observing Partner A. When time is up, I ask for a moment of silence and for everyone to take a collective breath.*
>
> *Then Partner B speaks. After both have shared, I ask them to remain silent, breathe mindfully, and feel their body temple.*
>
> *Part 2. For one to two minutes, Partner A speaks again, but this time sharing things they love and care about, things that bring them joy and exuberance. Again, after the allotted time, they stop, breathe, and feel. And then Partner B takes their turn.*

Every time I offer this exercise, the discovery is the same: Our body acts as a biofeedback machine for our emotions. We feel what we speak and think into existence, and the more animated and energetically we speak and share these thoughts, the more we feel them in our bodies. As your self-awareness grows, it will help you stay focused on life-enhancing thoughts and actions because your body will provide both large and subtle clues. However, be aware that uninterrupted, constant negative and self-denigrating thoughts will turn your body into a petri dish, cultivating illness and disease.

The purpose of the exercise and the awareness it affords is this: We are never separate from our thinking or feeling. We are constantly created by means of our spoken word and our unspoken word. This is the whole reason for this book. Get to know who you are in a conscious way so you can focus your powers of co-creation in a powerful and positive, uplifting manner. As you question yourself about your inner landscape, all you learn becomes the path you walk upon toward your freedom.

You can try the above exercise alone by making a few alterations. Set your intent to grow your awareness of how your body reflects your feeling or thinking words. Stand in front of a mirror and set the timer for one to two minutes. Start with your out-loud bellyaching—a really good bitch session—and then go onto life-affirming ideas. Always stop when the timer rings and take a cleansing breath in between. And always end with the uplifting focus. Throughout, feel your body. (This is a great exercise for coaches to suggest to their clients to help grow their self-awareness.)

Then in the name of inquiry and contemplation, ask yourself a few revealing questions:

* How does my body feel when I am spewing venomous and toxic thoughts and judgments? Take note. Pay close attention to where you feel it in your body.
* How does my body feel as I share uplifting, positive thoughts and ideas?
* What reminders would I like to set in place to stay focused on my chosen direction?

Let these awarenesses support new thinking and speaking habits. When necessary, start anew—over and over again. Don't expect quick results. Some of these thinking habits have been yours for a lifetime.

THE ROLE OF SILENCE

Silence can feel intimidating or soothing depending on your level of experience, emotional maturity, and sense of safety. My intention in using the term *emotional maturity* is not to judge but to provide a tangible way to recognize how easily or challenging you navigate through life. Spiritual and emotional maturity have become integral in our social and professional worlds like never before. These aspects measure how capable we are in navigating life. Fear or discomfort with silence might be a clue to some of your unhealed pain. If you find it difficult to feel safe even in your home, you will not be able to let your guard down and allow growth in. This is a definite invitation to heal what's in the way. You do not want to be at the mercy of this kind of fear.

Your sense of safety greatly influences your focus in the world. Learning to embrace silence, both externally and internally, will support you in feeling safe wherever you go. When you can be in silence without creating stories or entertaining worry, you will automatically feel safer in the world. Your true authentic self, unhindered by old stories and pain, would bask in your own company—wow, imagine that.

Practicing silence regularly will support you in various aspects of life. It will help you sleep better, feel at ease during power outages, and help you be comfortable when alone unexpectedly. I once had a student who thanked me for facilitating a silent retreat because it was there that she learned not to be afraid during a power outage. She discovered untapped inner strength.

Silence will support all your inner reflections. Amid quiet, you will find answers, ideas, creative inspirations, and new self-confidence. This silence will have a direct impact on your spiritual growth. How? Because what matters most in this world has nothing to do with what we own, how much money we make, or our level of education. It is the spiritual nature of your life. You will never be poor or limited when you create a relationship with your inner world, living at the heart of your inner landscape—that is, your authentic self that is You.

I believe so much in the power of silence to grow and expand your consciousness that I wrote and self-published a book encouraging people to organize their own weekend silent retreat.

Initially, self-inquiry can feel anything from mildly challenging to downright painful—that is, until you fully realize that your self-inquiry and traveling your inner landscape is the shortest path between the life you are living and the life you desire to live. This practice is *not* about trying to manifest money and success in your outer world. It is all about rearranging your priorities and thinking habits until they completely align with your highest values and your desire to live a life of stunning authenticity free of self-judgment and self-doubt. This investment of time leads you to dancing in the middle of the dance floor with music generated from your heart, needing nothing outside of you and no one else's approval.

Yes, go to the middle of the dance floor and get away from the edge, where it is safe and boring.

Can you see that? Can you imagine yourself dancing to your internal song of strength and satisfaction? We all have an anthem, a feel-good song. If you don't, get one. Identify a song that you must sing and dance to every time it plays. (Another great coaching tip: Have your clients identify their powerful feel-good song and suggest they play it daily. Music moves our heart and soul in a way nothing else can.)

Now see yourself alone in the middle of the dance floor, arms raised, eyes closed, shoeless, loose clothes that move and sway as you move and sway, topped off with a smile that says, "I have learned to love myself as I am and as I am not—no reservations. I am now committed to looking within courageously and enjoying all the benefits to be had."

As you practice the art of contemplation, you will find yourself in a mystical mode of receiving inspiration and guidance that seemingly comes out of nowhere. This happens because when we sit and contemplate long enough, we are surrendering our conscious thinking and allowing ourselves to be receptive. This is not unlike what happens because of meditation. It is the result of sitting still long enough to capture the inspiration that is always swirling around you. Most of us are so busy running, working, and doing, attached to our opinions, that we become a moving target, unable to catch the ever-flowing inspiration that seeks a ready vessel.

Think of it this way: Imagine seeing two people playing catch, regardless what kind of ball is being tossed. If they are both stationary, it is easy to aim for their receiver and easy to catch the ball, but the moment one of those individuals starts running around, the odds of throwing directly to them or catching the ball on the fly becomes increasingly more difficult. This is the same as sitting in stillness and assuming a position of receptivity.

There are some sweet assumptions that come with this practice, if you are willing to accept them. Once you sit to ponder, the unspoken assumption is that you are connected to the universal intelligence that flows through all things, *and* that you are worthy of being inspired and informed from it. How sweet is that? How sweet it is to answer the call from your soul to receive such good?

Similar but a bit more profound is the assumption that you are worthy of receiving this inspiration. Now this might sound presumptive on my part, but I have met too many students who were conditioned to not believe in themselves or their worthiness, and it was simply not true. When you sit to receive this wisdom, you are saying, "I am worthy." There is no greater gift to your spiritual authenticity than to know you are worthy.

Live your life like an open book for all the world to read.

I'd like to take a moment to introduce you to one of the greatest influences of my life. Every word you have read in this book exists because of this statement: ***Live your life like an open book for all the world to read.*** This was taught to me by my spiritual teacher, and I took it to heart. This statement became my true north, the guiding light to keep me acutely focused on healing and transforming who I was.

If the above statement is going to serve as your true north—then you must learn to love yourself as you are, without excuses or justifications for who you've been. It means you must forgive yourself for your errors and transgressions and leave any lingering guilt or shame on the altar of transformation.

And I share with you, in all honesty, there were some very necessary and radical changes I had to make to live this way. I was not living honestly at that time in my life. I was not a model of authenticity. My life was riddled with influences that I used to justify my sad, complicated, and often shameful behavior.

To live your life like an open book—for all the world to read—will require you to make several significant shifts. Your true north, the guiding light that lives at the core of your being, will illuminate the areas where your life may be misaligned or in quiet contradiction to your deepest values.

To live life full-out may call for radical change—changes that will be prompted throughout the pages of this book. For me, that path was long and layered. It took years of practicing forgiveness, doing deep shadow work, and learning—slowly, painfully—to tell the truth. Truth-telling was the hardest. In my youth, telling the truth could have been dangerous. If you were raised in a home that didn't feel safe, you probably understand exactly what I mean.

Once I was fully committed to living this way, everything unlike it had to go and a new path needed to be laid out. Eventually, everything I did was in service of living my life out loud, fully expressed, totally undefended, and gloriously alive. Every book I have written, every class I teach, and how I engage all who enter my life hopefully have benefited from my desire to never again lie, make an excuse, or explain my rationale. **Oh, the freedom that comes from living an honest life is so incredibly beautiful, so free, so easy.**

This is my dream for you as you read this book.

Imagine what your life would look like if you were always proud—not from an egoistic place, but from a place of knowing that you deeply invested in yourself, and your pure authentic essence became your new normal. Can you imagine always feeling safe and never again lying about who you are? Can you imagine that? I ask this question often throughout the book because it is your imagination that will carry you to the next expression of yourself that you desire.

Take some time to ponder your life minus all the thinking habits and self-judgments that kept you hidden. This is the same kind of experience that one has the first time they go on a silent retreat. The first half day and maybe even the whole day can be very uncomfortable for a first-time silent retreater, but once they settle into the silence, they start to feel a sense of relief that comes from not trying to display their personality and taking a break from their ego. Suddenly one can sense the stress and strain that comes with always having your personality be on.

A commitment of this kind will activate this phenomenon that we in metaphysics call *chemicalization*. Chemicalization is what happens when you set yourself on a new and powerful journey toward a new and transformed version of yourself. What you quickly experience is that everything unlike your desired outcome *must go*. Before it goes, it is suddenly in your face. It is likely that you have already experienced some of this as you have moved slowly through this book. For example, when you began to read the chapter on self-awareness, it is altogether possible that you found yourself in situations in which you were surprised by some thoughts you didn't realize you pondered. It can be an uncomfortable and contrary experience initially, but you soon discover that chemicalization is the shedding of thinking and being habits, or those things that do not support who you are choosing to be.

This reshaping of your being, while ultimately rewarding, requires a mature spiritual approach. At first, it may feel like everything is falling apart. But in truth, everything is falling into place. As you shed the layers that once blinded you to your beautiful essence, the process can feel disruptive. The key is to recognize that this transformation is natural, good, and clearing the way for you to live more purely, more freely, and more fully as the divine being you truly are.

POWER PRACTICES FOR SELF-INQUIRY AND CONTEMPLATION

- ★ Before going to bed each night, shut down all devices, turn off the lights, and light a single candle. Then just sit in silence for five to ten minutes, feel whatever you need to feel, and then take this silence into your sleep.
- ★ If you are someone who likes music or a television playing in the background, schedule times in your home *and* in

your car when you shut everything off for a period of time. Schedule this time at least once per week and up to many times weekly. In the silence a few things happen. First, you will begin to hear yourself think, you will finely catch that inner voice that needs to be heard. Second, you will be able to catch inspiration to support your creative self. And third, you will find relief from your personality. You might not realize it, but it takes a lot of attention and energy to keep being you.

* Lastly, when you are in conversation with another person, notice how learning to be silent has improved your ability to truly listen. You can hear what they are saying without forming an answer. The old you would wait for them to stop speaking just so you could jump in with a brilliant response. Silence cultivates great listeners, and great listening creates great relationships.

If you are serious about identifying your authentic self, voice, and thinking, go on a silent retreat. They happen all around the world. You will find everything from a three-day to a monthlong silent retreat; some are free and some for a fee. A simple online search will reveal a plethora of options.

As silence becomes a benefit to your thinking and feeling habits, take note of your new tendencies of thinking. You will want to monitor the flow of your thinking throughout your day because life has many distractions, some small and some large. But because you are now determined to live a life of spiritual authenticity, your self-inquiry and contemplations will reshape you into an individual ready to receive an abundance of love, most specifically self-love (see path 12).

One last thought. When we take ownership of our errors, we are no longer victims of society's judgments. When we understand who we are through deep contemplation, we stand tall, no longer living at the mercy of outside commentary or gossip.

Self-inquiry and self-awareness, strengthened by powerful self-talk, create a foundation for a new way of being.

DANCE WITH ME IN YOUR IMAGINATION

Imagine a world shaped by individuals who have raised their self-awareness through honest self-inquiry and have the courage to truly know themselves.

Imagine a world where, from our families to our workplaces to our neighborhoods, we gather—not to judge or gossip, but to engage in meaningful conversations about our personal growth and expanding awareness.

What a beautiful world that would be.

JOURNAL PROMPTS

Use these prompts, writing the answers in your journal. Please remember no editing, no judging yourself. Just write—freely and openly—without any limitations.

* Write about a time when you were really jarred by an interaction. Ask yourself this: What part of me reacted? What am I attached to or threatened by?
* What part of me needs to be seen and loved so I feel more empowered?
* Choose a current challenging life experience and ask yourself this: What do I need to change to land strongly on my own two feet?

* When I feel resistance, what am I learning about my needs, fears, or desires?
* How can I honor the truth of my emotions while remaining grounded in my highest self?
* What assumptions or beliefs am I holding right now that might no longer serve me?
* In what ways can I embrace the uncomfortable parts of this moment as an opportunity for growth? (Choose one specific thing to focus on.)
* What am I afraid to look at within myself, and how might facing it bring me closer to freedom?
* What part of my story needs to be rewritten so I can step more fully into my power?
* Who or what am I seeking approval from, and how can I redirect that energy back to self-acceptance?

A MOMENT OF APPRECIATION TO YOURSELF

Stop whatever you are doing, take a few full deep breaths, put your hand on your heart, and affirm, *I am profoundly moved by the realization gifted to me from sitting still. This practice is rewarding me in ways I could not have imagined. Each time I sit now, all my attention is drawn inward and away from the chaos of the outer world. Even after a short time of practice, I love how this has become almost instinctive. Quiet is now a reward that has changed my life.*

A SPIRITUAL MINDSHIFT TO UPLEVEL YOUR SELF-INQUIRY AND CONTEMPLATION

Oh, Beloved, my heart overflows with gratitude for this sacred calling—to step into the quiet, embrace the stillness, and surrender to the depths of self-inquiry and contemplation.

As I journey inward, I uncover wisdom where I once saw only shadows. In the silence of this moment, I allow myself to be sourced by the boundless genius of the universe, the same genius that has birthed modern miracles; composed the great poems, prose, and novels of the ages; and orchestrated the very rhythm of existence. That same genius moves through me, as me, and I open myself fully to its presence.

It is breathtaking to witness the brilliance that arises in the spaces between moments—the beauty of inspiration, the clarity of understanding, the expansion that comes from being fully present. I sit in communion with this divine intelligence, and I am moved; I am uplifted, stretched, and catapulted into a new, boundless way of thinking and being.

Through inquiry and contemplation, I evolve.

I am in awe of the limitless potential that is my life, and with deep trust, I surrender it to the quantum laws that make it so. And so it is.

A LOVE LETTER TO MYSELF

Dearest Self,

Today I offer deep gratitude for your willingness to walk the quiet, sacred path of self-inquiry and contemplation. It's neither the loudest path nor the easiest, but it is one of the most powerful.

You have dared to ask the deeper questions: Who am I beneath the stories? What do I truly value? What stillness lives beneath the noise? These questions have not always come with quick answers, but still, you've asked them with openness and courage.

Rather than rushing past discomfort or grasping for certainty, you've chosen to sit with mystery. You've allowed silence to be your teacher. In still moments, in the pages of your journal, in the spaces between your thoughts, you've listened.

This practice, this turning inward, has cultivated wisdom. It has shown you truths that no one else could give you. You are discovering your own inner compass and learning to trust it.

Thank you for your devotion to reflection. Thank you for meeting yourself again and again with honesty, patience, and grace. May your contemplative heart continue to guide you home.

With deep reverence,
Me

REMEMBER TO BREATHE

Take a breath, make it from your belly, and breathe so that all the lobes of your lungs are full. Do this for a count of six, hold that breath for a count of four, then release it for a count of six.

Feel the presence that comes from mindful breathing. It is also a great reset and will help you manage your anxiety.

Let's Conclude with These Affirmations

- ✶ I give myself permission to pause, reflect, and ask the deeper questions.
- ✶ I trust that every answer I seek lives within me, waiting to be revealed.
- ✶ I honor the journey of not knowing, and the wisdom that emerges through presence.
- ✶ **I demand to be me—without excuses.**

PEARLS OF WISDOM

We began with self-talk and self-awareness because that is what is necessary to grow on, but now you get to take a more active role in redirecting your life toward your authenticity by learning to ask empowering, self-inquiring questions.

When you have a sense of curiosity and wonderment about who you are, and you ask questions to uncover the best parts of yourself, you will become free to be expressed.

Make sure all your questions are designed to uplift you. Let us never again ask the question, "What's wrong with me?" Instead, let's remember to ask, "How glorious a life can I have?" And, "What would happen if I always danced like nobody is watching?"

4

DISMANTLING THE INNER JUDGE

The Path to Heal Your Self-Criticism

What you do speaks so loudly that I cannot hear what you say.
—RALPH WALDO EMERSON

Description of Self-Criticism

Self-criticism is the result of having an undisciplined mind while misusing the law of co-creation, which is how we create ourselves and our world. Self-criticism eats away at our confidence and self-acceptance.

Here Is a Quick Start Option

Beginning this moment, commit to never again criticizing yourself, unless it is to improve upon a new skill you are learning. Listen to your mind and to what comes out of your mouth; make sure those words sync up and make sure they are life-affirming.

After you begin a steady practice of self-inquiry, you might run face-first into all the self-concepts that have been standing in your way. While this is uncomfortable, it is a necessary part of your journey. Until you recognize just how much you have a habit of getting in your own way—and how you unconsciously undermine your brilliance through self-criticism—you'll have no idea of all that has been feeding your self-sabotaging ways.

You know the phrase *breaking the glass ceiling*. Most of the world looks at that glass ceiling as being imposed upon them, but in truth that glass ceiling is self-imposed and girded by your incessant self-criticism, self-judging, and faultfinding. Maybe it's not you. You might be the only person in the world whose voice does not drag you down, but because you picked up this book, I feel certain that you are one of us—those whose thinking habits have been negatively impactful, causing you all sorts of upset and disappointment.

To break this glass ceiling and all other illusions of limitations in our lives, we must retrain our thinking and redirect it to things that lift and encourage us. We must **stop** all the self-doubt by not fueling those doubts.

Many of your self-doubts are born of your unexpressed fears. Your fears feed your self-doubt, and your self-doubt feeds your fears like a snake eating its own tail. This pattern, while necessary to break, is not readily easy to identify because the influences are old and born of our domestication, as we adopted the hypnosis of our family. These conditionings seem real because, until now, you didn't consider questioning them or the reality they proposed.

As we continue to journey within to find and express greater resources toward freedom, we will begin to develop a new idea of ourselves, and it will be beautiful because you are beautiful. Please walk this path not with a tendency to self-condemn but with a longing for freedom. Don't just walk—strut, strut like you're wearing a crown and clothes made of the finest silk.

Here is the thing: We cannot reach freedom without first acknowledging what freedom looks like to us as an individual, and what stands in the way of our experience. The path will be revealed, but it must be traveled with courage and curiosity. We must journey through our past and who we have been to a certain degree. We cannot go around it. There is no shortcut; walking straight through the middle is ultimately the shortest path.

To challenge what is real, we must first identify these thinking habits and our behavioral habits. It is altogether possible that you actually believe the limiting bullshit in your mind and haven't learned to question your status in life. As I said earlier, if there is a glass ceiling, let's be clear, you put it there by not challenging it. Unless you live in a country with a very clear caste system, you must question everything and begin by questioning your own self-limiting self-concepts because under all that activity is a source of power waiting to be expressed.

All self-criticism is held in place by layers of societal conditioning and family alignment. This alignment—what Don Miguel Ruiz refers to in *The Four Agreements* as domestication—is both stealthy and deeply invasive. It has shaped who you believe yourself to be so subtly that most of you thinks it's real and unchangeable. But it's not. It's conditioning, not truth. And the moment you recognize that, the process of liberation begins.

Pay attention to your heart's yearnings. And begin to challenge the thoughts and ideas that have held you captive.

Self-criticism is born from the limiting universal beliefs that most of the population shares albeit quite unconsciously. They are the perfect storm of limiting beliefs: These beliefs are "I am not lovable, not worthy, and not enough," and oh yes, there are more, many more, but these seem to be shared across all socioeconomic and educational boundaries. Self-criticism and associated behavior do not care if you are rich or poor, educated or not.

These beliefs hover underneath the fabric of our essence, hidden so well because of our collective agreement. This agreement is not conscious, which is what makes it so powerful. It continues to exist like a deadly secret hovering in the corners of our subconscious minds. Our subconscious mind is a collection of all that we have ever experienced. It remains living there influenced by all your experiences, like a hoarder not wanting to throw anything out. It bides its time like a predator waiting to pounce on your confidence just when you have decided to break free.

Our ego never wants to let go of control, and returning to your authentic self, the parts of you that cannot live in that expanded atmosphere must go, and this threatens our ego. We should also note that our ego does work on our behalf, whether we recognize it or not.

Changing our internal dialogue to one that lifts and frees us is the single most important habit for us to attain right now. We all live with loud and identifiable inner messages, often negative ones, but to truly refine our thinking, we have to listen to the voice *behind* the voice. There are many layers of voices, so we must take time to train our listening. Many of these layers of voices were adopted from a wide variety of places and influences. We adopt ideas by what we've heard, what has been said to us, including all the subtle, mostly unconscious unspoken messages, through both stagnant marketing and social media.

We have measured ourselves long enough using standards that we did not create but adopted, and since we never learned to question them, we thought them to be real, resulting in the habit of limiting thinking and so much self-criticism and self-judgment.

Often a student or client sits before me, and I can see they have given their power away to their conditioned self. It saddens me how the masses have never thought to question that inner voice. This is especially true for women. Women, the givers of life, the ones who make this world possible and yet act like undeserving second-class citizens. I had considered writing this book for women only, but being the mother of three beautiful sons and now two grandsons, I prefer that my legacy of writing benefit them also.

If these self-limiting, self-criticizing habits only applied to women, then the world would be in a totally different place. The world is a clear reflection of leaders—mostly men, mostly white—who wield their power, filtered through their insecurities, wonder why most of their decisions are not easily embraced, and continue to cause a culture of distrust everywhere throughout society.

When we do not love ourselves enough, when we judge and criticize ourselves, we are rejecting ourselves and all the best parts of us that would make a world of peace, love, compassion, and empathy possible. This condition that I am speaking about is a breeding ground for white supremacy and imperialism. These can only exist in a culture of toxicity born of self-hatred, desperation of power, and greed.

PUTTING SELF-CRITICISM ON NOTICE

I wish I could tell you, with full honesty, that I never criticize myself anymore. And to a degree, that statement is true—but only because I've learned to catch the thoughts. That inner critic still lives within me. It's like that annoying little cousin you love but don't always like—you know the one. The one who wants to sit next to you at dinner, who insists you play with them during the holidays, who needs your undivided attention. Yes, that one. Endearing and irritating all at once.

That critical voice has been groomed over decades, fed by my inability to recognize it early on and retrain it. So even now, well into my sixth decade, that voice still has battery life, no matter how many times I've tried to power it down. I could beat myself up about it—I could criticize myself for being self-critical—but come on, that would be ridiculous.

I'm here in this book with you because I'm one feisty and determined Jersey girl living on the East Coast of the United States—and if you don't know about this personality type, let me tell you: We are driven. And I am driven—not to kill off that inner voice entirely, but to make damn sure I'm not living at its mercy. I am driven to free myself from that incessant, sometimes downright obnoxious voice.

Here's what I know: That voice was cultivated over time. We've talked about this already—how it gets shaped by parents, culture, religion, teachers, media, and even subtle societal cues. And at this stage in my life, I've come to see that a lot of what still triggers it isn't even real anymore. It's old messaging that seeped in through the cracks of living.

Another trait of being a Jersey girl? A quiet but constant inner competition. We're scrappy. We love our sports teams, our hometown musicians, especially Bruce Springsteen, Frank Sinatra, Jon Bon Jovi, Queen Latifah, and Whitney Houston. We love our actors Meryl Streep, Jack Nicholson, John Travolta, and more. We take pride in our tomatoes, cranberries, and blueberries. We root hard for our people—and maybe, just maybe, we compare ourselves to others a little too often. Living where I do, you learn to broaden your shoulders. People are loud. They cuss. They're direct. But honestly, most of what's said to me from the outside rolls right off.

The real damage? It comes from within. It's that residual voice in me that never got matured through self-knowledge. I can easily dismiss someone else's opinion of me (at least most of the time), but the voice that lives in my psyche—the one that still tries to eat away at the part of me that wants to make a difference in the world. And here is the kicker: I also know that it does this to keep me safe from harm, just like the other parts of my ego that work overtime to keep me safe. Weird, huh?

If you're reading this book, I know you have a dream. A dream of being free from that voice. A dream of living beyond those self-limiting beliefs. And guess what? You deserve to be free, just like I do. **Some part of you is wondering: *Does it get any better than this?***

This book is an invitation to walk that path together.

In my classes and here in this book, I've encouraged you to find a friend you can share this journey with. Someone you can speak honestly with about the voices in your head. Because here's the thing: The best way to raise your self-awareness is to give it away. Help someone else recognize their voice and yours will get quieter. **Don't miss out on this gem.**

Find a friend with a dream. Someone who's stuck because they're not catching the inner critic. Share this book with them. Start a book study. Read together. Because the more you talk about this, the more it becomes real, and the more it loses its power.

Here's my biggest concern: not the people who hear the voice, but the ones who don't. The ones who move through life on autopilot, never questioning the status quo. The ones who accept mistreatment from their boss, their spouse, or their kids because they've never examined the silent agreement they made with the voice that told them, "This is just how life is."

Before you can grow something new, you have to know what's already there. So, put your self-critical voice on notice and say out loud, "I'm coming for you."

Even the quiet whispers—the ones that once seemed so reasonable—declare, "I'm done listening." This moment in your life is about declaring full agency over all your thinking. This book is dedicated to everyone like us who is ready to take their power back.

I've gotten a little fired up writing this chapter, and I like that. No, actually, I love that. That's the part of me that knows my power. It's not just a Jersey thing. It lives in the hills of Tennessee, the mountains of Colorado, the streets of Chicago, and the homes of women across the Middle East who have been silenced for generations.

THIS IS YOUR MOMENT

Put that inner saboteur on notice and start the blog, write the book, pick up the paintbrush, record the song. Say the thing. Take the risk.

And just to circle back to one of the most elementary, but sneaky, tactics of the self-critical voice—it's subtle. Sometimes so subtle, you don't even notice it. You see a job listing and think, *Oh, I'm not quite qualified*, even though you totally are. You meet someone you're drawn to but stop yourself from saying hello because something whispers, *You're not enough.* You don't challenge it because it's quiet. It sounds *reasonable.*

But let me tell you: That voice has stolen opportunities. It has blocked love, joy, abundance, and connection. It has talked you out of dreams before you even gave them breath.

So, let's be clear. We hear it now. And because we hear it, we can heal it. Together. (Mic drop!)

CAPTURING THE VOICE OF THE INNER CRITIC: ADDITIONAL JOURNAL PROMPTS

- What does your inner critic *sound* like?
- Is it your voice or someone else's? A parent, teacher, culture, or collective fear? Describe its tone, style, and favorite phrases.
- What specific things does it say to you most often?
- List recurring criticisms, doubts, or dismissive thoughts that play on repeat.

* When does it usually show up?
* Identify the moments when or environments where this voice gets loud. Is it before taking a risk? After a success? When you're tired? Around certain people?
* What did it cost you? List experiences, relationships, or opportunities that this voice has talked you out of or sabotaged.
* What does this voice believe it's protecting you from?
* Even the inner critic has a function. What fear or pain is it trying to avoid (failure, rejection, embarrassment, disappointment)?
* What do you *know* is true about yourself that this voice ignores?
* Write affirmations or truths that reflect your *real* self, not the voice of fear.
* If your inner critic were a character, how would you describe or draw it?
* Give it a name, face, outfit, or personality. Is it playful or serious? Personify it so you can talk to it.
* Write a letter to your inner critic.
* List what's changing. Be fierce. Be funny. Be truthful. Thank it if you want but reclaim your authority.
* Write a declaration of agency.
* Start with: "From this moment forward, I no longer . . ." or "I now choose to believe . . ."
* Write yourself a new agreement.

And love on yourself as you write this agreement. Make it bold and ironclad.

POWER PRACTICES FOR SELF-CRITICISM

To shift your self-criticism, you must commit to daily mindfulness. Release any rigid expectations and, instead, focus on

one day at a time. Growth is not about perfection—it is about presence.

Here are some simple yet powerful practices to support you on this journey. There are many because this habit is so incessant, and we all need to transcend it.

- Observe your inner dialogue. Throughout the day, pause and notice the tone of your self-talk. Is it harsh, judgmental, or discouraging? Gently redirect it with kindness.
- Reframe negative thoughts. When you catch yourself in self-criticism, ask, "Would I say this to a dear friend?" If not, reword it with more compassion.
- Practice self-compassion. Speak to yourself with the same love and patience you would offer to someone you cherish.
- Schedule a daily gratitude check-in. Each morning or evening, write down three things you appreciate about yourself—qualities, actions, or even small efforts.
- Engage in mindful breathing. Take a few deep breaths when self-doubt creeps in. Ground yourself in the present moment rather than spiraling into past regrets or future worries.
- Create an affirmation practice. Choose empowering statements like "I am enough, I am learning and growing," or "I release judgment and embrace love." Repeat them daily.
- Limit comparison. Social media, workplace dynamics, or even family expectations can amplify self-criticism. Remind yourself: "My path is my own, and I honor my unique journey."
- Embrace mistakes as growth opportunities. Instead of seeing missteps as failures, view them as teachers. Ask, "What can I learn from this?"
- Make self-care part of your daily ritual. Whether it's movement, meditation, art, or rest, nourish your mind, body, and spirit. This will encourage you to approve of yourself as you take action.

* Surround yourself with supportive voices. Be mindful of the people, books, and media you engage with. Choose influences that uplift and inspire rather than reinforce self-doubt. Always choose to be with people who love you as you are. And stop tolerating people who are unkind or abusive. You deserve better.

Remember, transformation happens through small, consistent shifts. Choose one or two of these practices and integrate them into your daily life. With time, patience, and self-love, you will rewire the way you see yourself—one mindful moment at a time. We are here to break those old habits.

DANCE WITH ME IN YOUR IMAGINATION

Imagine a world where people are so rooted in their own worth that judgment has no place in their world, where self-love replaces insecurity, and kindness becomes second nature. Imagine a world where differences are met with curiosity instead of conflict, where families could hold opposing views yet remain united in love and respect. Imagine waking up each day with a mind free from the weight of self-doubt, allowing you to move through life with clarity, confidence, and deep inner peace. **IMAGINE PEACE.**

JOURNAL PROMPTS

Write freely in your journal without editing or judging what you write. The freer you are with yourself, the more the wisdom will rise through you.

* Write about a time when you felt truly authentic and free from self-criticism. What were the circumstances, and how did it feel?
* List three qualities you love about yourself. How can you nurture these qualities in your daily life?
* Describe a situation in which you overcame self-doubt. What did you learn from that experience?
* Imagine your life without self-criticism. How would your relationships, career, and personal growth be different?
* Identify a self-critical thought you often have. Challenge its validity and replace it with a more empowering belief.
* Reflect on how self-compassion can transform your inner dialogue. How can you practice self-compassion daily?
* Describe a role model who embodies authenticity. What can you learn from their approach to self-criticism?

A SPIRITUAL MINDSHIFT TO DISMANTLE YOUR SELF-CRITICISM

Empowered by that which has created all that I see and all that I experience, I lean into that power, and I am fortified by it. For some, it might be called Love; it might be called Beauty; it might be called God; it might be called Spirit. But for me, it is the Intelligence that creates and re-creates, and this is what I lean on and in to. I am one in every way with this universal magnificence.

And on this day, I cease using my thinking and my language to criticize myself. I now elevate my attention, my language, and my thinking to be available to be lifted and inspired. I rise up through a spiritual evolution, and this is expedited when I stop finding myself wrong—when I cease the criticism. Instead,

I turn my attention to the holiness of my being, for I was born of the One and incarnated into this life fully ready to accept my good.

On this day, I declare that I use my faculties to lift myself up and to give permission to everyone around me to do the same. Yes, I model a life devoid of self-criticism.

I am grateful for this call to transform and release this word into the Law that acts upon it and makes it so. And so it is.

A LOVE LETTER TO MYSELF

Dearest Self,

Today, I pause to honor the incredible progress you've made on the path from self-criticism to self-kindness. There was a time when your inner voice echoed with harshness, quick to judge, quick to tear down. But you've done the brave work of softening that voice—and I see you.

You began to notice the tone. You questioned the old narratives. You dared to ask, "Would I ever speak to someone I love this way?" And in asking, you began to shift.

Little by little, you turned down the volume of the inner critic and turned up the voice of compassion. You've learned to pause, breathe, offer yourself the same tenderness you so easily give to others. You've begun to speak to yourself as a true friend—one who is loving, honest, and kind.

This transformation didn't happen overnight, but your steady willingness to release old habits has made all the difference. You've replaced judgment with curiosity, shame with grace, and harshness with patience.

I celebrate you, dear Self, for choosing a new way—one

rooted in love. May you continue to be your own safe place, your own soft landing, your own greatest ally.

With pride and deep affection,
Me, the you that you have chosen to be

A NEW RESET

Today I stop finding fault with myself. Today I cease picking myself apart only to leave my heart in pieces. Today I begin to alter my attention to that which I find myself doing right and to ways that I am thinking right. Right meaning to ways that I lift myself up.

I now begin to look objectively at my life to discover that parts of me are absolutely beautiful.

REMEMBER TO BREATHE

Sit somewhere quiet and for five minutes allow your self-criticisms to come to mind. With each thought, breathe a deep, mindful breath and affirm to yourself—with each breath—"I am more than this thought."

Let's Conclude with These Affirmations

- I cease the war within and give myself permission to soar.
- I release perfectionism and choose progress, grace, and growth.
- From now on, my voice, both inner and outer, is a powerful reminder of my beauty.
- **I demand to be me—without excuses.**

PEARLS OF WISDOM

I hope I have done my job thoroughly and have convinced you to never again criticize yourself. I'm not saying that you should not assess your life and make improvements, but I am saying with absolute conviction that you should never again be tempted to say a word against yourself. Deciding to make change or to heal or to expand some aspect of your life is great. But to beat yourself up and to criticize yourself and to tear down your essence and your heart is simply not OK. So please, dear reader, make your inner voice, your outer words, and your contemplation all synchronized to free up the authentic power of who you are.

5

STANDING IN THE SACRED NOW OF YOUR BEING

The Path of Self-Is-Ness (Beingness)

Caring for myself is not self-indulgence, it is self-preservation, and that is an act of political warfare.

—AUDRE LORDE

Description of Self-Is-Ness

Selfishness usually sparks judgment because most people think of a selfish person as someone who is completely self-involved and self-serving. For the purpose of this book, I want to retrieve this word to imply someone who is seeking to serve the Self that lives within, and going forth I will refer to *self-is-ness* as a powerful choice.

Here Is a Quick Start Option

The next time you find yourself wanting something, ask yourself these questions: Am I harming anyone by wanting this ___________? Will I feel good about acquiring this? If the answer to your first question is no, that's great. Go ahead, as long as it does not cause harm. If your answer to the second question is yes, then congratulations. You are on the path to living the life you desire without greed or manipulation.

* * *

What if *selfishness* became *self-is-ness*? Can you see how this would change so many of our perspectives? It is fascinating to me how easily we as humans can be conditioned to be a certain way. As a woman, I have become increasingly aware of how I have been domesticated to be a certain way—to put everyone first before me, to have fewer expectations for myself, and give of myself even when I have nothing left. Gratefully, through the focus and practices presented throughout this book, I managed to detach myself from the matrix and find out who I am authentically.

While this conditioning has been in my bones my whole life that I am meant to serve others, to do for others first, to give until it hurts because then I will know that I have given enough. Let's challenge that idea together, let's challenge it while respecting the conditioning of mothers—yes, mothers—because they birthed a new life into this world through their loins. The perspective of mothers about how to give, how much to give, and who to give to first is skewed by their natural conditioning to bring life into this world. It is as if giving birth brings with it a contract for a life of overgiving and overdoing.

Let's take a look at what happens to mothers and, yes, fathers, because the natural order of things does impact this conversation. People who are parents have a natural tendency to give to their children before giving to themselves, and I find it appalling at the number of articles that claim self-care should be higher on the list of mother/fathers/parents. If the one reading the article is living their self-empowered authentic life, they will just ignore the subtle comparisons and very subtle criticisms. But we know the planet is filled with people living at the mercy of other people's opinions; and when these articles are common in every magazine or splashed throughout social media in memes encouraging people to care for themselves first, it is a slap in the face, almost disrespectful and unappreciative. Often, they are left feeling like their parenting tendencies are wrong and they are not enough.

I want to make sure that while looking at the idea of being healthfully self-ish, I do not want to take away the love and sacrifice that comes when caring for another. In a very sacred way, the act of parenting is the highest call there is, and I will not be part of leaving the loving caregivers of the planet feeling anything other than amazing about their contribution. As a mother and a grandmother I would not trade one moment or one act of care that I have given to my children and grandchildren. I will always love and honor this sacred role.

There are elements of the self-care fad of this current culture that is akin to what I might call *blame porn*. I often wonder if those writing these blogs are parents or if they have ever been responsible for caring for another, or if they are parents whose pendulum swung so far in the direction of self-denial, that they are angry at the world. Yes, you can go too far and completely deny your own needs, that does happen, but let's not criticize those who choose to put their children before themselves. We all get to choose, and must live by our choices.

The purpose of my work—my courses, and all that I write as an author—is to support my students and readers in moving toward balance. When you are in pain, swinging the pendulum in the opposite direction is not balance; it is overcompensation. True balance looks like giving of yourself from the heart, knowing that your soul is satisfied by the love and service you offer—while also being self-aware and responsible enough to recognize what is happening *through* you, so that your self is nourished just as much as those you care for.

Now that I have gotten that out of my system, I feel a bit better. A good rant is healthy sometimes and I am just codependent enough—and proud of it—that I choose to protect those who care and those whose life expression and profession is about caring for others—like teachers. The same care should go for teachers, nurses, and hospice workers, in addition to really good coaches. All of these roles are powerful and meaningful.

Yet there are occasions when this role does go awry and could benefit from a bit of redirection. If our caregiving is the result of our conditioning and is not a result of our self-love and self-appreciation, it is possible that we are giving beyond our ability to care for ourselves. It is possible that you were taught to give so completely that you have been left a shadow of who you are meant to be, empty and uninspired to live a life that pleases you or frees up your creative juices.

Let us be honest here, selfishness when it is ego-based and centered on our lack, can be destructive. You will be more equipped to recognize the signs when you know what to look for. Some of these tendencies and behaviors are aspects you see displayed in life, books, and movies. None of these will surprise you, but it is likely you never thought of them as being selfish.

Here are some examples of selfishness when we are less aware:

Being blind to another person's needs happens when we are so self-focused that we do not recognize how much serving our own needs exclusively can harm another person and at the very least harm our intimate relationships. While there are personality types that are the very definition of selfishness, this behavior is often not obvious to the one displaying it because they have not learned to strip away their conditioning and they are unaware of their personal impact upon others. This is a clear example of being selfish and lacking a sense of empathy.

When one's attention is about getting their own needs met, there is a tendency to manipulate others to accomplish these goals. This will usually cause the one being manipulated to mistrust them, which then causes the one displaying selfishness to ramp up their efforts to get what they want. It is a horrible but common cycle for those who are either unaware or who display this psychological disorder.

Greed is one of the most pervasive and toxic displays of selfishness and it is at the heart of the inequity and disparity happening here in the United States. Greed is blinding—so much so that it is confused with a healthy participation in capitalism. Capitalism itself contains some innate issues, but capitalism, when displayed through individuals who are greedy and not self-realized, becomes a source of issues for the masses. Take a look at our banking system, our health-care system, and corporate greed. Greed is made possible when one's needs are projected everywhere outside themselves. Greed is selfishness on steroids.

Another way that selfishness displays itself is in leadership. When someone refuses to compromise, collaborate, or find consensus, they aren't leading. Instead, they are being a boss, one who can easily be threatened by self-realized and independent individuals. Conflict will always arise when one does not open the door to sharing ideas and collaborating. This kind of leadership is not sustainable.

Hijacking a conversation is such an annoying and selfish habit—one that I am particularly irritated by. Let me explain, in case you aren't familiar with this label. You're sitting with someone, sharing a story about something that just happened—like getting a flat tire on a very fast and busy highway. Suddenly, the listener jumps in and says something like, "Yes, that just happened to me the other day," and then proceeds to take over the conversation without letting you finish. This usually happens because the individual who jumped in doesn't know how to truly listen and doesn't care.

Now, because I like to find the balance in all things, let's consider why those who are selfish—excluding those with a chemical imbalance or a mental health issue—are selfish to begin with. Why? Why is this unhealthy characteristic present to begin with? It goes right to the heart of not feeling enough or not feeling seen, loved, or appreciated. When one is hungry, they will walk over whoever is in their way to be fed. Needy people struggle to be satiated through caring for themselves, so they think they need a resource outside themselves.

Their intense need blinds them to their surroundings and their impact on others. But we need to look at these individuals not with disdain but with compassion, through the eyes of love, because while their behavior has some hard and unfortunate outcomes, it is a sign of how empty they feel, which is sad.

If you have been accused of being selfish, then I encourage you to look inside yourself and take an inventory of the number of unmet needs and expectations you are trying to navigate. Be gentle with yourself, because the last thing you need is to judge yourself even more. Maybe you are hungry because you walk around feeling empty. This is not cause for self-criticism; this is a call for self-love. Only then can you peel away this layer to get to your authentic self. We can only give from our fullness. We can only give when we are certain that we are a child of this beloved universe with a birthright of glorious good.

But so many of us are walking around empty, a mere shadow of ourselves, seeking love and approval in the unhealthiest places and ways. This is what leads to the selfishness we see around us. Our goal here is to return to a state of fullness, which is a deep and profound connection to everything that surrounds us: all people, all of nature, and all of this earth's inhabitants. Only then can we give freely and generously.

I care deeply for people who are selfish because I know what is actually happening, but it does take a skill to look past this behavior to see the emptiness. If you continue this journey with me here and maybe with my forgiveness and shadow work, you, too, will find such a deep and profound love at the heart of your being that you, too, will be able to have compassion for those who the world most criticizes.

WHEN SELF-IS-NESS IS HEALTHY

Self-care is not an act of selfishness. Self-care is a statement of caring for the mind, body, heart, and emotions to be fully realized and to give from a place of fullness. As we know, you cannot give from an empty cup, which of course is the danger of parents that never take care of themselves and then resent those they are giving to.

Healthy boundaries are essential for self-care and sanity. Whether a boundary is seen as wise or selfish often depends on the perspective of the person labeling it. Just like the saying "Beauty is in the eye of the beholder," so, too, is the interpretation of our choices. A judgmental or critical observer might label someone's boundary as selfish, while someone who values self-awareness and self-respect will likely see it as wise and loving. Boundaries are not walls; they are sacred markers that protect your peace and give you permission to simply be. Sometimes a boundary can be as simple as saying *no* to an invitation you would have previously automatically accepted.

A question that I live with always in my adult life is this: Can I value and honor my soul as it needs to be expressed and freed so completely that I am willing to disappoint another to do so? This might sound harsh, but the gifts of serving my soul have proven out. I am more honest, live with greater integrity, and am by far more present to individuals when I do say yes and commit to something. Serving my soul will never hurt me, it will only and always strengthen you and how you show up in the world.

Pursuing personal self-growth, which means you put time aside for studying, reading, and possibly retreating, can be judged harshly by one who thinks that caring for the self is a selfish act. But when you ask your soul what it needs and then pursue that need with a class, a course, a workshop that leaves you inspired and excited is a loving way to care for yourself. Taking the time to learn a new skill, hobby, language, or travel to a new place—all of these things grow you. All of it makes you a more interesting person, and all of it will leave you feeling satisfied within yourself in a beautiful way.

If you have the habit of trying to get your needs met by placing your expectations upon another without consideration of your impact upon another, you can fully expect upset and conflict. But, to express your needs and to inquire with others about whether or not your needs can be met is an incredibly empowering thing to do. You will want to ask for your needs with a soft heart and an open mind, because the answer might be no.

Seeking solitude is a beautiful and advanced way to feed the self. Few people truly understand the value of a solitary or silent retreat, but once you take the plunge into the world of silence and experience the relief that comes from not having to be your personality, you will be changed forever and you will yearn to return to that space.

Taking yourself seriously enough to invest the necessary time to understand yourself and to feed your quiet or your creative side is a beautiful and generous thing to do. People who have known me for a long time would not guess that I am one who yearns for silence, but I do. Silence is the only opportunity I have to hear what is living deep within my inner landscape.

When you find your authentic rhythm, you will always be pleasantly surprised. Writing this book on authenticity was a task far greater than writing my other two books. When I wrote about forgiveness and shadow work, I already had documents and outlines in place. I'd been teaching those courses for years, so the material was already started. This book was born from concepts I had been teaching intuitively, but they were ideas I had not yet put down on paper.

Accepting the invitation to write this book was incredibly intimidating. I had to dig deep to believe in myself, cultivate confidence, and find words that matched how I view this process. I feel good about the result—but the journey to get here was full of self-doubt, followed by moments of pulling myself up only to run headfirst into doubt again . . . and then lifting myself up once more.

While writing the book, I also decided to teach a course on authenticity. And let me tell you, I learned so much through teaching it and from the incredible women who said *yes* to joining me in that beta course. I watched the students open up to self-realizations and uncover their own authentic ways of being. However, I wasn't just teaching; I myself was transforming, too. As I guided them, parts of me burst wide open. I found places where I hadn't been fully honest with myself. And I chose, again and again, to live in authenticity.

This wasn't a fun journey, at least not at first. But in the end, I felt lighter, more open, and more confident in my ability to rise up and answer the call to be bolder and more fully expressed. I'll forever be grateful to my publisher for inviting me to write this book. My confidence grew as I let out the Jersey girl in me. And wow, has that helped me live more and more authentically. My audience sees it. My students see it. My family sees it. And for all of that I am deeply grateful.

POWER PRACTICES FOR SELF-IS-NESS

Here are some simple and wonderful ways to fill your heart and soul, so your selfishness becomes self-is-ness: a beautiful and generous version of yourself.

Acts of kindness and generosity and expressions of gratitude are the clearest and quickest way to feel full. Once full, you will feel compelled to give because it will become clear how much this satisfies your soul. To benefit from these practices, you will want to pay attention to your somatic reactions. You see the reward of generosity is how it *makes you feel* in addition to how it makes the receiver feel. Remember, the body tells the truth.

- ✶ Begin with a simple practice. (This works really well at home with your partners and children.) Write notes of appreciation and acknowledgment using little sticky notes. Remember to acknowledge your family for a variety of things, including when they do things that they are expected to do, like chores. Then, they'll appreciate being noticed when things are going right. We all want to be seen; this little habit will give them that.
- ✶ Send thank-you cards—yes, actual paper-with-a-stamp thank-you cards whenever possible. The reward for you and for the recipient is large.
- ✶ If you happen to work in an office, try this little trick. A small gift like a handmade bar of soap, an individually wrapped brownie or cookie, a cigar, or something else you can imagine. Wrap the gift, take it to your office, and leave it on the desk of someone who can be cranky sometimes *without* letting anyone know who gave it. Watch what happens next as the receiver looks around to wonder who the giver is. Or you can take it further and give something to every-

one in your office and watch their smiles. Of course you must leave something on your own desk, so they don't know it's you. The key here is anonymity, that is where the magic happens. (This works great with your neighbors also.)

* If you dine out, tip your server more than is expected. Watch their face and feel the magic.
* And one mindful practice to incorporate: breathing. Yes, I know you are breathing, but are you conscious of your breath?

Right now, stop what you are doing, allow your eyes to close, and simply pay attention to your breath. Just sit and feel the breath as it enters your body, feel your diaphragm expand and, on the release, feel your shoulders begin to relax. Conscious breathing will help you change your relationship with and awareness of your body.

DANCE WITH ME IN YOUR IMAGINATION

Imagine your home, your extended family, and the world around you so full of life, love, and vitality that everyone feels naturally compelled to give from their overflow.

Picture a community energized by generosity—where giving isn't a burden but a joyful expression of abundance. In this space, collaboration and cooperation flourish effortlessly. Now imagine that flow of goodness moving *through* you or with you, as a powerful channel for love, connection, and grace.

What a beautiful world that would be—and how wonderful it is to know it begins with you.

JOURNAL PROMPTS

Write freely in your journal without editing or judging what you write. The freer you are with yourself, the more the wisdom will rise through you.

- ✶ Describe a time when you acted out of selfishness. What motivated your actions? How did it make you feel afterward?
- ✶ What unmet needs do you have that cause you to feel selfish or needy?
- ✶ How would your life change if you fed your self-is-ness and not your selfishness?
- ✶ What have you missed from being self-focused and what might you gain as you practice being a source of good and generosity?

A SPIRITUAL MINDSHIFT TO UPLEVEL YOUR SELF-IS-NESS

In this beautiful and glorious moment, I surrender all that I am and all that I think I want to be to make space for the divine intelligence and vibration of love to be my one and only reality. I am forever expanding, to the degree that I accept and allow this essence of good to be my essence of good.

I declare that I am ready—ready to feel the fullness of my being and to give from that fullness. I am ready to know, without question, that I am seen, loved, and supported by all elements around me, never needing to reach outside myself for completion. No person, no job, no possession can fill me. My fullness, my deep satisfaction, is the result of learning to lean into the ever-active, universal sea of life.

As I embody the giver of good—through acts of kindness,

generosity, and compassion—I expand even more, and from that fullness, I give again. The isness of my I Am is stunning as I transcend old ways of being and embrace the infinite possibility of me.

From this deep and sacred place, I express my gratitude for how sweetly and swiftly the universe responds to my spoken word. With unwavering faith and conviction, I allow this new reality to be mine. I shift my mind open to a new version of me.

And so it is.

A LOVE LETTER TO MYSELF

Dearest Self,

Today, I honor you for walking the path of Self-Is-ness—the path of simply being who you are, without apology, without performance. This is the path of wholeness, where you no longer try to become something for someone else but instead stand rooted in the truth of your own being.

You have learned that honoring yourself doesn't mean separation or selfishness—it means alignment. It means listening inward before seeking outward. It means showing up as your full, beautiful, complex self, without shrinking or shape-shifting to fit in.

There was a time when you doubted this wholeness—when you questioned your voice, your needs, your place. But not anymore. Now, you're learning to take up space with grace. You're allowing yourself to want what you want, to need what you need, to feel what you feel—all without guilt.

You are learning that just being is enough. That you don't have to prove or perfect to be worthy. That your presence is powerful because it is real.

I celebrate you for embracing this truth. May you continue to walk in the fullness of your being, honoring the sacred gift of your self—exactly as you are.

With deep love and unwavering respect,
Me

REMEMBER TO BREATHE

Every time your phone rings, use it as a reminder to breathe and accept yourself as you are. With each ringing of the phone, you will pause, breathe, and say to yourself aloud or silently, "I am worthy of being wonderfully alive."

Let's Conclude with These Affirmations

- I give myself permission to put myself at the top of my list.
- My presence matters. My needs matter. I matter.
- My essence is perfect, as I am.
- **I demand to be me—without excuses.**

PEARLS OF WISDOM

It is possible that this chapter might be the most challenging one you've read yet in the book, especially if you are a parent or a caregiver, because those individuals who are always looking out for someone else are often the most guilty of not caring for themselves.

Society, with so much conditioning, has taught us to put other people first, even when it causes us discomfort. But I challenge that belief, and I encourage you to put yourself higher on the list of priorities in your life. Then you will begin to give from your overflow and not from an empty well.

You deserve to care for you.

6

WALKING THE PATH OF FORGIVENESS, THE PATH TO FREEDOM

The Path of Self-Forgiveness

The most common way people give up their power is by thinking they don't have any.

—ALICE WALKER

Description of Self-Forgiveness

Self-forgiveness is the act of taking responsibility for one's actions and then choosing to love themselves enough to release the energy caught up in the shame and guilt of their errors and transgressions. This leads to loving oneself in an open and free way.

Here Is a Quick Start Option

When you catch yourself judging, gossiping, complaining, or placing blame, forgive yourself immediately. If you speak against yourself, forgive yourself immediately. Do this daily and as quickly as possible.

SELF-FORGIVENESS LIVES AT THE HEART OF BECOMING AUTHENTIC

If you don't know this about me yet as the author of this book, I am a very strong proponent of forgiveness and have written a very well-received book on the topic called *Forgiveness: A Workbook for Emotional and Spiritual Freedom*.

Self-forgiveness can be more difficult than forgiving anyone else that you have encountered in your life, because we have been conditioned to be extremely hard on ourselves.

Self-forgiveness is difficult because we are so judgmental about ourselves, even more than we are judgmental about others. Maya Angelou is believed to have once said, "Forgive yourself for not knowing what you didn't know before you learned it." An abundance of your self-worth is held hostage by self-condemnation. When you finally choose your freedom over self-condemnation, you will find the path that will lead you back to yourself, your fully beautiful, fully expressed authentic self.

I consider myself to be an expert on the subject of forgiveness, as I have been writing about and teaching it for a couple of decades in addition to my expertise garnered by surviving a hard life. Forgiveness was my savior, the savior of my soul, and continues to be. While this chapter is about self-forgiveness, we must start our journey with releasing others. We begin with others because it is the low-hanging fruit and it is in our face as we find ourselves annoyed, pissed off, and sometimes righteously so.

In case the thought in the back of your head is: *I thought self-forgiveness is all that matters?* Yes, however it is a both/and. It is never an either/or; it is always a both/and. We must forgive ourselves while also forgiving everyone in our lives and the people around us. Every time you withhold your forgiveness, you create a restriction of energy through your life.

Because I feel a responsibility here to acknowledge that our world—and likely your life—has been stained with the pain of cruelty. Our history is all the evidence we need to see how ruthless some people and leaders can be, and how desperate our planet is for healing, equanimity, and radical transformation.

Here's what I also know: **We are not bound by the past.** We are not doomed to repeat cycles of harm. Each of us has the power to shift, heal, and rise above the weight of history and become something greater—individually and collectively.

It begins with awareness: the willingness to see things as they are. It deepens with forgiveness, the courage to release what no longer serves us. And it flourishes with action, the daily commitment to love more, judge less, and be the presence of peace where once there was pain.

Our world is longing for us to show up differently, to rewrite the story with more compassion, more justice, and more love. The question is: Are you willing?

As you become a container for this level of forgiveness, you increase your capacity to look inward and free yourself. Yes, you might be able to begin with self-forgiveness and work outside, but my experience tells me otherwise. This way of being will create an emotional muscle, a mental atmosphere, and a readiness to forgive yourself and be free from the condemnation you have carried.

To fully practice, we must look at guilt, how we adopt it, and how we can use it for our growth. You, my dear reader, might be one who has experienced abuse, survived dangerous situations, or been the victim of downright cruelty and bigotry. Often, even when one has survived hard experiences caused by another, you continue to carry guilt in your heart as if you were responsible for what happened to you. As unreasonable as that might sound, it is what happens. It happens because we lost our way and forgot our beauty and our value.

Even if there were no other reason to forgive yourself, I encourage you to do just that: Forgive yourself for suffering, for playing small, for not prioritizing your good, for not believing in yourself, and for allowing yourself to be influenced and formed by the collective societal lies told to us. You deserve to be free. Your self-forgiveness will lead to self-kindness, radical self-care, and radical self-tenderness. (This last term was used by a friend and colleague, Christie Hardwick, for her book title *Radical Self-Tenderness.*)

More on How to Implement Self-Forgiveness

On the following pages, I provide some authentic power practices and journal prompts to encourage your mindfulness, but nothing—no amount of reading or course-taking—is more important than setting a strong intention. **Intention** is the conscious direction of thought, energy, and action toward a desired outcome or purpose.

While on this path returning to your authentic self *might be* long and winding, and triggering at times, a solid, well-spoken intention toward a particular outcome is the single most important act you can set in motion. Your intention—or as I like to call it, your "why" (I'll explain more about your why below)—if strong enough, will guide you toward your freedom; because if your intention is strong enough, you will be empowered to constantly readjust your sails to arrive on the horizon of your heart's desire. For me, that intention is freedom. Freedom from all discord and freedom to embrace the fullness of my being, my authentic self.

Your why is the reason that you set for moving your decisions and focusing in a certain direction. Your why needs to be short, simple, and compelling. My why, for example, is this: I forgive so I can be free and will walk through a baptism by fire to do so. Write something that grabs your heart and attention.

Consider using this dialogue (below) daily or along with the ritual that I suggested in the authentic power practices earlier in this chapter. Please remember that you can't free yourself from the past until you free yourself with love and self-compassion.

A New Inner Dialogue

- *I am now willing to forgive myself for all my errors, faults, and transgressions. I am willing to forgive myself for doing what I did based on my limited consciousness at the time. I forgive myself for not taking care of myself enough, for not prioritizing my own sanity over taking care of others.*
- *I am willing to forgive myself so completely that there is nothing left inside me to stain my heart with shame or guilt.*

A couple of things to consider as you proceed: Guilt, while being an uncomfortable emotion to experience, has a purpose. That purpose is to let us know when we have crossed beyond the line of our own moral code. Guilt is not something to get rid of but to honor and use as a self-guiding system to return to our empowered self. Simply, it is a sign that we wronged someone or ourselves.

Shame is a more complicated emotion because it brings with it a sense that we are wrong, which of course is not true. We adopt shame from our own decisions and from a system of abuse. There is nothing wrong about you, but that knowledge may not be enough to release it.

And remember that self-love, self-forgiveness, and self-acceptance cannot be contained energetically in the same place as self-judgment and self-condemnation. This is the time to choose in favor of yourself with focused intent.

MAKE YOUR LEGACY GLORIOUS

What we received from our family is our lineage, but what we leave to our children and those under our care is our legacy. I encourage you to take your legacy seriously. A healed and whole you—one who questions reality and seeks to uncover its vast mysteries—is one who will recognize the importance of every single interaction you have with those under your care. For parents and direct caretakers, this is quite obvious. If you haven't learned this yet, it is important to realize that those you influence are not just listening to what you are saying, but they are also watching your every move.

Whether you like it or not, you are modeling life by your words and your interactions. People are always watching us. This does not mean that you should change anything about who you are to get attention or approval, but it does mean that you are a model of your beliefs and those beliefs are demonstrated through our actions.

If you are blessed by being a parent, grandparent, godparent, teacher, or a caregiver, your role in the lives of those under your care leaves a lasting impact. Some of your influences are wonderful and some are not. Every parent knows the feeling of witnessing their child doing something they don't approve of. Suddenly, you realize that they got that from you. That is an ouch that many of us live with.

This is another example of how being aware of your values can guide your life and your decisions. If leaving a healthy and prosperous legacy matters to you—and you declare that now—it becomes a compass for your behavior and choices. When you stay conscious of your values, your actions naturally align, much like a sailboat that requires a steady hand and watchful eye to stay on course. Small, consistent adjustments will lead you toward the life you envision. With focus and intention, you can create a legacy you're proud to leave behind for your children and grandchildren.

As a longtime minister, I have facilitated many a memorial celebration in my time, and what was obvious at each one was the level of influence that particular individual had in the lives of so many people. Some of those influences were not obvious to others and very likely not obvious to the one who passed away. We are not just what we intend, we are also what is perceived by others, including our unconscious ways of behavior.

I had the good fortune to also conduct many a life celebration for both family, friends, congregants, and my most valued spiritual teacher. And during those memorial services, I was always reminded about my own values, who I wanted to be, and how I wanted to build my legacy. Not one time can I remember a memorial service that did not include stories about the deceased that many people in the room would respond to with either tears or laughter.

For me, writing this book is part of that legacy.

DON'T LET YOUR LEGACY BE A REFLECTION OF YOUR PAIN AND TRAUMA, LET YOUR LEGACY BE YOUR PROFOUND ESSENCE.

In truth, I want love to be my legacy more than anything else.

Much of the world lives at the effect of what was, meaning the past. This is why studying history is so important. You know the saying "Those who cannot remember the past are condemned to repeat it" by George Santayana? Children and the young in our care are not conscious or aware enough during their most impressionable years to know just how much they are adopting the habits of their elders.

If you're living a conscious, self-aware, and authentic life, congratulations—you're embodying the beauty of the very essence that created you. If you reach a point in life when you're ready to take responsibility for your role within your family and society, you step into a space of self-empowerment. And it's from this place that your legacy will shine.

Even if you are not in direct contact with the young ones in your family, you are not off the hook. As I mentioned above, grandparents, godparents, aunts, and uncles are being watched all the time, and your family will tell stories about you. They will laugh, at your expense possibly; they will cry if you touched their lives; and they will be grateful for who you have been.

I have incredibly vivid memories of family members who we hardly saw and yet I was influenced by the stories told about them. You live in the lives of your grandchildren, nieces and nephews, and godchildren, even if you're absent. They are watching you from afar. How you show up to family events, if you show up, and what you carry into the room leaves a lasting impression. When we don't feel important, we are not in touch with how much impact we do have on the lives of those around us.

Your legacy, to any degree, matters. YOU MATTER. Who you are, how you are, what you say, and how you say it lands in the hearts and minds of those around you. As you continue to read this book, use it as a source of inspiration to be you, to be the version of you that you feel really good about.

Things to Ponder

* What are the most impactful memories I have of my family?
* How have I impacted my family?
* What is my legacy? What would I like my legacy to be?
* Have I left love behind, or have I left fear and doubt behind?
* What values and principles do I hope to pass on to future generations?

* How have my actions and choices influenced those around me?
* What are the most important lessons I have learned, and how can I share them with my family?
* In what ways have I contributed to my community and the world at large?
* What stories from my life do I want to be remembered and shared?
* How have I faced and overcome challenges, and what can others learn from my experiences?
* What kind of impact do I want to make, and am I living in a way that aligns with that vision?
* How do I want to be remembered by my friends, family, and community?

Be honest with yourself. These questions are not meant to spark guilt or shame. They are meant to wake you up to who you are and who you choose to be, and to encourage you to choose more wisely. Ponderance and contemplation is a beautiful spiritual practice, to see through the clouds of confusion to the clarity of truth. And, by the way, if your answers cause you upset—that's good. That is an indicator you're discovering something new about yourself. But also remember to forgive yourself immediately and thoroughly, because you did the best you could. As your self-awareness grows, you will always do better.

As you learn to love and accept yourself as you are, you will model that behavior also, and as you heal and show up authentically, I can promise you the doors of acceptance will swing wide open.

Another Exercise for Your Expansion

Letter writing is one of the most effective and lovely ways to see what is resting on your heart and hiding in your mind. I am suggesting some particular focuses for these letters. Should you choose to accept this assignment, please do so while sitting in a quiet, familiar place so you can feel safe and calm. I would also suggest that you keep these letters private, as this will ensure you feel safe to be 100 percent honest and authentic.

Write, my friends. Write for your life; write for your heart. Lastly, feel free to include people who are alive and those who have transitioned.

* Your ancestors: Begin by first writing a letter to your immediate family, your ancestors, or your adopted family. Acknowledge what you learned from them and, if appropriate, release some of their heavy influences and forgive them if you feel ready to do so.
* Your children: Write a separate letter to each of your children. Speak of your dreams for them and what you would like them to know about you when you are gone.
* Your future descendants: Write a letter to your future grandchildren or great-grandchildren. Share stories about your life, the values you hold dear, and the legacy you hope to leave behind. Offer wisdom and advice to guide their future.
* Your world at large: You are a child of this beloved universe. You were gifted reign over the heavens and the earth, and hopefully you are doing so consciously, compassionately, and kindly. But let's be clear: There is no private good so stake your claim as to how you would like your legacy to impact the whole.

POWER PRACTICES FOR SELF-FORGIVENESS

Forgiveness is not a onetime thing. There can be no grand, sweeping efforts that will take care of all the reasons simultaneously that one has to forgive. The suggestions that I offer here as practices are expressed in greater detail in my *Forgiveness* book. Start here, but if you want to take it deeper, read my book and give yourself the gift of forgiveness, especially self-forgiveness.

* Set your intention to be free. Based on the previous reading, ponder your intention to forgive yourself, which will

afford you a freedom to express yourself fully. Create it, write it down, and commit to it.

* Begin by taking an inventory in two different categories. First, make a list of all the people in your life that you believe harmed you in any way. List everything from small offenses to painful betrayals. Second, list all the things you have done in your life that you feel you need forgiveness for. Be thorough.

Once you have these lists, start to forgive through your spiritual practices, mindful intentions, or the writing of letters to release all individuals who have caused you harm. Then, most importantly, forgive yourself for any extended suffering. Forgive yourself for giving your power away to those individuals, which will allow you to take your power back.

Then begin to forgive yourself daily, forgive yourself for all your errors and transgressions. Be kind and have compassion for yourself through this process. As you begin to free yourself from these accusations, you will find a gentle, loving freedom and a new path to your authentic self.

* After you have made progress on the practice above, every day, check in to see if you have to forgive someone or yourself for anything that happened that day. Keep your forgiveness list up-to-date.
* Depending upon your spiritual leanings, meaning whether you have a god in your life by any name or a higher power that you turn to for advice, mindfully ask this authority if there is something that you need to know or someone else you need to forgive to keep the mirror of your soul clear and clean.
* The most important part of these practices is this: Do it daily, using the personal inventory that you have already written of all your actions. Continue to release yourself from your errors while also learning from them. Practice extreme kindness and keep track of your actions in your journal, so you can learn from them.

- Be humble and ask for forgiveness if it seems appropriate, and make amends as long as you can do so without causing more harm. Free yourself by taking action.
- Write a letter of forgiveness to yourself, from the most compassionate, loving, and wise part of you. What do you need to hear?
- Create a ritual to support your experience. While a ritual can never replace the work of raising awareness and getting conscious, a ritual when mindfully created and implemented can offer a sweet and loving opportunity for you to satisfy your heart, and your intention.
    - Once you have been practicing self-forgiveness for a while, consider taking the inventory you created about your errors and ceremoniously burning it—safely—while speaking a word of gratitude and release.
    - For twenty-one, thirty, or forty days—all meaningful amounts, depending upon your point of view—light a candle each day while speaking a mindshift or affirmation that you write for yourself. Or you can use the one offered at the end of this chapter.

DANCE WITH ME IN YOUR IMAGINATION

Imagine a life in which past mistakes no longer weigh you down. Imagine the freedom of loving someone fully, even when they falter. Imagine a world where forgiveness is practiced openly and without shame—where ego takes a backseat to healing. Imagine the love that could flourish between us if we focused more on each other's hearts and needs rather than our flaws. And imagine a world in which forgiveness begins within, self-forgiveness is the foundation, and love naturally follows. *Now it starts with us.*

JOURNAL PROMPTS

Write freely in your journal without editing or judging what you write. The freer you are with yourself, the more the wisdom will rise through you. Ask yourself the following questions:

- What past mistake or regret still lingers in my heart? If I could speak to my past self with love and compassion, what would I say?
- What would change in my life if I truly forgave myself? How would I show up differently in the world?
- If my best friend made the same mistake I'm holding against myself, how would I respond to them? Why do I struggle to offer myself the same grace?
- What unrealistic expectations have I placed on myself that keep me trapped in guilt? How can I release them?
- What lessons have I learned from the choices I once judged myself for? How have those experiences shaped me for the better?
- In what ways have I already grown past the version of me that made those mistakes? What proof do I have that I am evolving?
- What part of me is afraid to let go of guilt? What does that guilt falsely convince me of, and what truth do I want to replace it with?
- If I believed, right now, that I am worthy of forgiveness, how would that shift the way I treat myself today?
- What small act of self-kindness can I practice today as a symbol of my commitment to forgiving myself?

For Your Contemplation

Because self-forgiveness is key to freeing yourself to be authentic, here are some additional prompts. They are quotes from some well-known teachers and leaders. Again, remember that the purpose of self-forgiveness as it relates to your authentic self is this: When we are angry at ourselves, carry fear of being found out, doubt our value, or have shame for our actions, this leads to hiding. We create a false face, one that we believe the world will accept, and in turn reject our parts by creating a shadow self.

Forgiveness of others and forgiveness of self is more important than you can imagine to returning to your authentic place of power within your inner landscape. Please move slowly through this chapter, returning to it as often as you need.

Here are quotes from great teachers. Read them. Contemplate upon them. And journal your responses.

* Mahatma Gandhi: "The weak can never forgive. Forgiveness is the attribute of the strong."
* Martin Luther King Jr.: "Forgiveness is not an occasional act; it is a constant attitude."
* Lewis B. Smedes: "To forgive is to set a prisoner free and discover that the prisoner was you."

While this is one of my favorite quotes, I always find it necessary to translate it—not only for myself but for anyone who lives a more spiritual than religious life.

> ***For if you forgive others their trespasses, your heavenly Father will also forgive you. But if you do not forgive others their trespasses, neither will your Father forgive your trespasses.***
>
> **—MATTHEW 6:14–15**

For if you forgive all others who have caused you harm, you will feel free to release them from your heart and mind. But if you do not forgive them, you will suffer by your attachment to your opinions, judgments, and the innate suffering that accompanies these hurts.

Father represents your consciousness. *Trespasses* are any errors or mistakes. In metaphysics, *sin* means mistakes. This is telling us that all of life is a reflection of our consciousness, as we refer to it: as within, so without. Your dedication to forgive yourself will guide and govern how you respond to others and will impact all your relationships near and far.

A SPIRITUAL MINDSHIFT TO UPLEVEL YOUR SELF-FORGIVENESS

One life, one spirit, one essence of good flowing through me in all moments of my life. This life is power, is love, and it transforms me every time I open myself and become available to it. It expresses as my life in the most beautiful and stunning ways.

This one beautiful and powerful Life and I are one now and forevermore.

The more conscious I am of my value in this life, and the more aware I am of the freedom that I desire and deserve to express, the more I declare my willingness to practice true self-forgiveness and self-compassion. I am not limited to who I have been, to anything that has ever happened to me, or my mistakes and transgressions. Today, right now, I commit to forgiving myself completely.

Anywhere in my subconscious where there has been a collection of memories, stories, pain, and most specifically where these elements have created beliefs that have informed my life and my choices—all of it—is right now uprooted, cast out, neutralized, never again to have any power or influence over me. This pain will never again determine who I am.

I have one identity—God. I have one authority—God. In this

One, I rest and live and have my being. Today, in the most conscious way possible, I choose to forgive myself, my past, my mistakes. I forgive myself for any harm that I have ever perpetrated upon another. I forgive myself for any harm that I have ever perpetrated upon myself. I forgive myself for lingering in the suffering of all my self-judgments. Today, I declare that I am DONE! I choose FREEDOM. I choose to LOVE myself as I am, and as I have always been. I love the all of me. I recognize the innocence that lives within me and always has. I recognize that there is a place within that has never been hurt, harmed, or injured in any way—this is the truth of my being.

I am free, free to be love, free to be fully expressed, free to be open to receiving a bounty of good that I have never known before this moment. With bountiful and unending gratitude, I surrender this word to love and to law!

And so it is!

A LOVE LETTER TO MYSELF

Dearest Self,

Today, I hold you in deep tenderness as I honor the courageous journey you've taken on the path of self-forgiveness, and your choice to find freedom through forgiving others.

You have faced the moments you once wished to forget: the mistakes, the regrets, the words unsaid or said too harshly. You've turned toward them, not with shame, but with a willingness to understand. That alone is an act of healing.

You've begun to loosen the grip of old guilt. You've seen that holding yourself hostage to the past does not serve your transformation. And so, breath by breath, you've chosen to let go. To erase the past, and to release its weight. To free yourself.

In forgiving yourself, you've created space for gentleness, or softness, for the kind of grace you've always deserved. You've remembered that you are human—learning, evolving, growing. You now know that you are not the sum of your missteps, but the sum of your efforts and willingness to shift.

I celebrate your willingness to love yourself anyway. To embrace the wholeness of who you are, scars and all. May self-forgiveness continue to open your heart, lift your spirit, and remind you of your beautiful, unbreakable worth.

With compassion and reverence,
Me

REMEMBER TO BREATHE

Take time to sit quietly, someplace where you are alone so you can free yourself to feel what comes up as you take time to ponder and breathe. Set your intention for this time to one where you choose to forgive yourself. With each full, mindful inhalation, say to yourself, "I forgive myself for all my transgressions," and with each exhalation, say to yourself, "I am free."

Be gentle here, and love yourself through this breathing practice.

Let's Conclude with These Affirmations

- ✶ I now give myself permission to forgive myself for all I have carried—knowingly or unknowingly.
- ✶ I release shame and open the door to healing.
- ✶ I now focus on freedom and am wildly rewarded.
- ✶ **I demand to be me—without excuses.**

PEARLS OF WISDOM

There is no person alive today who does not deserve to forgive themselves for all their transgressions and to allow for healing and transformation. I don't encourage you to forgive yourself just to let yourself "off the hook"; I encourage you to forgive yourself so you can find a new direction, new energy, and new enthusiasm for change and transformation. You have been ordained to be fully expressed, and that cannot happen until you forgive the self. As you move through your day, if a feeling of self-denigration and self-criticism comes up, forgive yourself for whatever the cause of those thoughts are and free yourself to love yourself and others more generously.

7

LEARNING TO TURN YOUR COMPASSION INWARD

The Path of Self-Compassion

To love ourselves is to love nature. We can't be good to nature if we are not good to ourselves.

—THICH NHAT HANH

Description of Self-Compassion

Self-compassion is the art of being gentle with oneself as they reflect upon the entirety of their life. Instead of finding fault and blame, they look at themselves through the eyes of love and understanding.

Here Is a Quick Start Option

Self-compassion calls for extreme kindness and gentleness. When your inner voice sounds like self-condemnation, stop immediately, put your hand on your heart, and say in a whisper to yourself: "Be gentle, my friend, you deserve the love, patience, and compassion that you show others."

This is the time—especially this far into this book—to realize that you need to stop treating yourself with disdain while simultaneously being kind and compassionate to those around you. Stop putting yourself last. Stop taking the crumbs.

Compassion is so often focused outward and rarely focused within. As I have already stated many times before, please be gentle with this deep dive. When you first learn the steps to a new dance, it might cause a bit of nervousness; but the more you practice, the easier it gets until you finally just know the dance with great confidence. Once you actualize self-compassion, you will no longer be able to tolerate being unkind to yourself or accepting unkind behavior from anyone else.

As you raise your standards, it will impact how you engage the world around you.

Part of self-forgiveness is self-compassion. While most of our internal criticism is unconscious, as we challenge our adopted belief systems and turn our attention inward, it is a great time to be gentle and loving with ourselves. We need to stop suffering for our unconscious choices. Through self-compassion, you will begin a gentle journey of freeing your spiritual authentic self. The gentler you are, the more willing you will be to look inward, and experience needs to be felt so all can grow from it—all your thoughts and feelings are critical to being authentic. Your humanity is as important as your spiritual essence.

People often respond to strong emotions by labeling them as scary, but this leads individuals to avoid those emotions. I suggest, instead of treating them like blocks to your authenticity, think of them like cobblestone blocks, building a path back to your authenticity. Once healed or even mildly shifted, a new, open, and accepting attitude occurs. Transform every block into a cobblestone merely by choosing to see it differently. You are the one who creates your life, after all, so do it through refocusing and choosing wisely.

To have self-compassion is to say, "I am worthy of the same acceptance and understanding that I choose to give others." Read that out loud again. Pay attention to how your body responds to this new idea.

This new habit will feel like stepping into a new skin. You'll look in the mirror differently and hold your self-inquiry and self-assessment with greater gentleness. In time, you'll see it's something that truly works on your behalf. The beautiful reward for cultivating self-compassion—and learning to listen to that inner voice, that quiet inner calling—is a warm tenderness that's been waiting for you all along. Until now, you may have ignored it, distracted by the constant chatter of the monkey mind, as the Buddhists say, and by the exhausting effort to fit in and seek approval from all the wrong places. And truly, any place is the wrong place if it lies outside of yourself.

It is interesting how quiet the wise voice can seem in comparison to that loud annoying voice that sometimes keeps you up at night. It is time to retrain your brain to listen for the inner voices that empower you. You can do this.

Let us remember that self-compassion is not yet a common phrase in our cultural vernacular. Terms like *self-forgiveness* and *self-awareness* are more widely recognized, but *self-compassion* often remains in the shadows. Many authors and teachers tend to collapse the concept of self-compassion into the idea of self-care. While they may share overlapping qualities, self-compassion operates on an entirely different level—a level that invites deep, internalized kindness and a radical acceptance of one's whole being.

Self-care may involve taking a break, getting a massage, or saying *no* to overcommitment. Self-compassion, however, requires looking inward with tenderness, especially when we falter. It is the practice of meeting our own pain with love instead of judgment, of softening rather than hardening in the face of our imperfections. It says, "I may have made a mistake, but I am still worthy of love."

This level of grace is not just healing—it's transformative. It dissolves shame, quiets the inner critic, and creates the inner safety needed to grow. In a world that often rewards harshness and productivity, practicing self-compassion becomes a revolutionary act. While it might not seem obvious, all efforts to love, accept, and approve of oneself is also a revolutionary act because as we shift from self-hatred to total self-acceptance, our world transforms, and we will begin to want these same advances for the people in the world around us.

Remember the story I shared in the introduction, the one about learning how to dance? Well, we each have within us a yearning to be free; and as you continue your journey back to your authentic self, you are going to free all sorts of aspects of yourself through embracing your truth and being gentle with yourself. Remember, the rewards are always freedom and joy.

This is what we are doing here: We are looking for those personal opportunities to be who we came here to be without seeking approval—it is the most freeing act possible.

To do that, we must begin with how we treat ourselves, especially in the quiet moments. Another word for self-compassion is *self-kindness*. While being kind to yourself might seem quite logical or normal, you have probably been quite rough on yourself, demanding more, and criticizing yourself. As you become more mindful, you will begin to change some of your thinking habits. And hopefully, you will become intolerant of habits that do not empower you.

Be honest: Are you tough on yourself? When was the last time that you judged yourself rashly when what you truly needed was a bit of TLC (tender loving care)? A couple years ago, I made a commitment to myself to cease talking to myself in any way other than with kindness. What followed was quite shocking at times. I discovered that I am often my worst critic and really needed to become very conscious about how I spoke about myself to others and to myself. Self-compassion is a call to be kind to yourself at all times.

This is the time for you to listen to that inner voice because this time around being on the dance floor will exist for a lifetime. Begin to retrain your brain now: Listen to what you say and what you think, and be kind throughout. Don't let yourself condemn your efforts or your failings. We all fail at times. Lessons learned from failing, while hard, are meaningful. Be gentle, be kind, be compassionate toward yourself.

Another way we confuse self-compassion is with self-pity, but it is not the same. Pity may seem like compassion on the surface, but it carries a subtle message of powerlessness. When we pity ourselves, we reinforce the idea that we are victims of our circumstances, helpless and dependent on rescue or external validation. Instead of attracting empowerment or solutions, pity tends to attract more struggle, neediness, and often, people who either want to fix us or feel superior to us.

Pity can also repel the kind of authentic connection we're actually longing for. While empathy says, "I see you, and I know what it's like," pity says, "Poor you—you're broken." It creates a gap instead of a bridge. When we dwell in self-pity, we energetically signal that we're not ready to rise, not ready to take responsibility, and not yet open to change.

As you can see, self-pity is not close to self-compassion.

You don't want pity; if anything, you want presence. You need compassion that reminds you of your strength, not your weakness. You need kindness that honors your humanity while calling forth your wholeness. You need to give this to yourself.

As we begin to practice self-compassion, we can expect to feel more resilient, manage stress better, and reduce some of our anxiety. This renewed focus will promote resilience and leave you feeling emotionally stable. Face it: It is the difference between trying to ward off a bully—yourself, in this instance—who is constantly picking you apart and preventing you from having a very best friend sitting on your shoulder and whispering sweet affirming ideas inside your head. It is often fascinating to me just how much self-abuse we learn to tolerate. As you move along this beautiful path toward your authentic self, may you find kindness and patience along the way.

It is a long and arduous job getting a grasp on the ways to cultivate the authentic self. While there are many paths leading you to your final destination, sometimes the paths cross. Self-compassion is one of those paths that bob and weave with self-care, self-acceptance, and self-love. As your journey continues, you will see that self-compassion leads to healthier self-esteem (also covered in this book) and it all culminates in a greater sense of self-worth (also discussed near the end of this book).

When you decide to take the path of self-compassion, there is a sweet yet powerful and unexpected benefit. That benefit is how it softens you and your opinions, opening your heart to others. When you are compassionate with your life and all that you have gone through to be who you are and where you are now, you will begin to empathize with others more quickly and more authentically.

When you start to have patience for the struggles you went through, you will begin to recognize the struggles of others, causing you to understand the woes of others without the judgment attached. As you know yourself better, you will begin to know others more.

Oops, I Made a Mistake

> *A quick personal share. About twenty years ago when I was serving in the pulpit of a spiritual community, I was walking through the sanctuary when I suddenly remembered that I forgot to call someone back after they'd left a message. My initial reaction was one of self-condemnation, beating myself up, and for about fifteen very long and hard seconds, I felt terrible. But then as quickly as that feeling came over me, I had a kinder and more compassionate thought and perspective about myself and I realized that I hadn't done it on purpose, nor would I want to. I chose to immediately forgive myself and simply apologized for delaying the return call. But as you can see, our condemnation is built in and so unconscious.*

Learning to recognize that domesticated and adopted voice from society and family and then turning it around is an incredibly loving act for yourself. It is radical because the United States is not well acquainted with this type of self-empowered individual and will often be intimidated by them. Care not, my friends; stay with your journey. Your light doesn't actually threaten others; in truth, the more you are authentically you, the more you give permission to others to be their authentic selves.

I don't know about you personally, but I for one have experienced many, many failures in my life. I have tried and not succeeded at so many things. And because I was in the pulpit for over twenty-five years, I failed publicly. I am avoiding using euphemisms for the word *failing*, purposely not replacing it with *challenges* or *opportunities*. This is a habit that so many spiritually-minded people rely on to avoid the subject. Failing is not a problem unless we do not learn from it, or we judge ourselves harshly for it.

Failing in and of itself is a very real human thing that happens. Not only is it OK, but it will also always be one of your greatest teachers when you learn to not be afraid of it; and when you commit to not condemning yourself, freedom is the reward. When you try something new, take a risk for a new project and reach for the golden ring, should you miss it, self-compassion is a beautiful way to recover, leading you to not be afraid any longer to try and try again. Failing can stop being something you are afraid of and instead be something you chalk up to your human experience. We all make mistakes or are imperfect. We all fail at times. Sometimes the fall is gentle and sometimes it is a total and complete disaster; but when you practice self-compassion, your recovery will be quickened.

As you learn to be compassionate about your efforts in life, including the errors and failings, you naturally strengthen your personal resolve. This is personal growth at its best. This Brené Brown quote, "Talk to yourself like you would to someone you love," is a most beautiful reminder that you deserve your own love and acceptance. (Self-acceptance and self-love are two other paths we discuss in this book.)

It is said that we have two brains: one in our head, and one in our heart. There is a lot of research being done to support the power of resonance between our head and our heart. The influence of the HeartMath Institute, a nonprofit organization with global reach, is dedicated to teaching methods of deep and profound head-heart resonance. With this in mind, it is beneficial for you to have some practices at the ready to be used in the moment when you feel tempted to criticize or condemn your behavior.

POWER PRACTICES FOR SELF-COMPASSION

- When you make a mistake, instead of criticizing yourself simply say *oops*.
- If you stub your toe, just care for it without calling yourself a name for causing the stub.

- Should you break something, know that all material things can be replaced and forgive yourself immediately.

DANCE WITH ME IN YOUR IMAGINATION

Imagine a world that you live in where you are surrounded by kindness. Imagine a world in which people who are kind to themselves are also kind to others. Imagine having affirming conversations with people who come together in connection and kindness.

JOURNAL PROMPTS

Write freely in your journal without editing or judging what you write. The freer you are with yourself, the more the wisdom will rise through you.

- What does self-compassion look like to you?
- In the middle of being tempted to find yourself wrong, what statement, affirmation, or mantra unique to you would help you to return to the path of self-compassion?
- Imagine the sense of relief that will come with your self-compassion and kindness and write about what that will feel like.
- If you spoke to yourself the way you speak to a dear friend in need, what would you say?
- Recall a past moment when you wish you'd shown yourself more grace.
- Write a letter from the most compassionate, loving version

of yourself to the part of you that struggles. What do these parts of you need to hear?

- ★ If you could fully embrace the idea that you're already enough, exactly as you are, how would that feel in your body (somatic focus)?
- ★ Do you still feel unworthy of your own love? How can you gently rewrite that story?

Sometimes you've got to say goodbye.

I had a student, an adult male who had a high level of integrity and self-confidence in the world until he got up in his years and began working for a person that he had very little respect for. (We always change the names, but for this purpose let's just call him Patrick.) Patrick needed a job. He needed an income and he had something to offer the person he began working for. He had wisdom and the experience of being a lifelong entrepreneur, but life had taken its toll on him and his confidence to a certain degree. So when he began working for this individual, it was great at first. He was treated with the respect that was to due him because he brought decades of entrepreneurial experience and wisdom. But over time his employer began to show signs of mental health issues, and this became problematic.

The stress of this toxic situation most definitely took its toll. After a lot of putting up with an intolerable situation, he finally decided to leave. On the day that he made that final decision and communicated that to his employer, he felt so free and tremendously different, and finally he could be his authentic self and not be part of the lies that he had to play into while at this job. You, too, deserve to make tough decisions that leave you empowered and happier.

A SPIRITUAL MINDSHIFT TO UPLEVEL YOUR SELF-COMPASSION

Recognizing the ebb and flow of the stunning universe that I live within, I also recognize the power of co-creation that lives within my being. I align with this power of co-creation, I accept it as a creative force in my life, and I allow it to express through me in the most beautiful and glorious ways.

It is with a gentle approach that I now practice self-compassion—a radical self-compassion. I am willing to take a compassionate approach to responding to life and to looking at myself in the mirror. I bring love and acceptance to myself in a compassionate way—the same way I would extend compassion to a dear friend. My act of self-compassion shows up in a variety of ways, but one of the most important ways is my ceasing to judge myself and my refusing to take responsibility when it is not mine to take.

I choose to focus on a gentle, loving, and compassionate point of view when reflecting upon myself and contemplating who I have come here in the world to be. With this soft and tender approach, I see tenderness in places within myself where I have not seen it before. I recognize that this tender way of being allows me to heal and grow in profound ways.

I am so beautifully moved by the call to be compassionate with myself. I have profound gratitude for this inspiration, and I release this sacred and holy word to the power that creates through me and as me. With abundant gratitude, I simply allow this to be so.

And so it is.

A LOVE LETTER TO MYSELF

Dearest Self,

Today, I celebrate your journey on the path of self-compassion, the sacred art of treating yourself with the same kindness you so freely give to others.

You have begun to speak to yourself with gentler words. You've learned to place a hand on your heart in the hard moments, to breathe deeply when things are too much, and to offer comfort instead of criticism.

You no longer demand perfection. You've started to see your struggles not as failures, but as invitations for tenderness. You've stopped pushing yourself through pain, and instead, you've learned to pause, listen, and soothe.

Your heart has become a softer place to land—for yourself. And that shift changes everything. I am proud of how you've embraced this way of being. It takes courage to be soft in a world that often asks us to be hard. But you are doing it. One breath, one choice, one kind word at a time.

May your compassion continue to bloom from within, and may you always remember you are worthy of your own love, every single day.

With warmth and admiration,
Me, the you that you have wanted to be

REMEMBER TO BREATHE

Life will always offer us opportunities to practice self-compassion. It is time to learn how to use your breath throughout the day by staying present. Whenever you are tempted to be hard on yourself or self-criticize, STOP. Take a breath, put your hand on your heart, and say to yourself, "I choose to be lovingly gentle with myself."

Let's Conclude with These Affirmations

- ★ I give myself permission to be kind, loving, and gentle with myself.
- ★ I embrace the messy, the magnificent, and everything in between.
- ★ I commit to my self-compassion without reservations.
- ★ **I demand to be me—without excuses.**

PEARLS OF WISDOM

While writing this book I had to admit to myself that this chapter on self-compassion was the most perplexing for me. I had no original concept of self-compassion. It was as if I had no sense of deserving this kind of compassion. My wish, want, hope, and dream for you, dear reader, is that you do not delay in embracing the concept of self-compassion. This is a very important practice, most specifically when it comes to your making mistakes or needing to forgive yourself. Self-compassion is a version of self-love that we all need.

8

LAYING DOWN THE ARMOR AND EMBRACING ALL OF YOU

The Path of Self-Acceptance

Talk to yourself like you would to someone you love.
—BRENÉ BROWN

Description of Self-Acceptance

Self-acceptance is the very beautiful practice of accepting oneself exactly as they *are* and as they *are not*. This should include all aspects of one's being, a practice that can feel radical but is freeing.

Here Is a Quick Start Option

Start this practice by having fun with it—keep the mood light. As you begin to grow your self-awareness and you catch yourself making some mistakes, just run to a mirror, look yourself in the eye, and say, "I love you as you are." Accepting your actions and tendencies is the first step to making the changes you want to make.

While I consider self-acceptance to be one of the most important tasks any human can take on, I am clear that most humans have probably never had a thought about it. Most people are so busy just being, they do not reflect back on themselves to see and measure how they are being. Who they are and how they react seems perfectly normal to them. But there is so much more of life that we can experience when we stop, look inside, and accept what we see—and enjoy the process.

This is the perfect time to take on the practice of self-acceptance because **when we love and accept ourselves with great abandon, nothing can interfere with our peace or shake up our grounding**. As we shed these very normal human, albeit limiting habits, another version of us begins to emerge from the newness. You might not know what you will look like in the end, just as a caterpillar doesn't know what is happening during the time that it is liquefied in the chrysalis. But both you and the caterpillar are created with the spiritual essence of what you're both called to be, what you were birthed to be. It was always within you. You are being called to be your fully expressed self.

"Accept yourself as you *are*, and as you *are not*." I have been teaching this for decades now, and everyone who hears it for the first time is taken aback by the second but very important part of the statement. In jest I will add that I will never be a five-foot, ten-inch blonde, so learning to accept what I am not is a survival mechanism; otherwise I would be walking around miserable all the time.

Learning to accept yourself exactly as you are is one of the greatest gifts you will ever give yourself. Learning to love the all-of-you—meaning every morsel of your being—is not only the most self-loving act one could take on, but it is a radical move in this world filled with companies and corporations spending billions of dollars in an attempt to hypnotize you into thinking that you should be thinner, taller, blonder, stronger, smarter. To not accept yourself is a painful injustice and is a disregard for the gift of your divine birthright. I wish I understood how we have gotten so far from loving and accepting ourselves completely. I would really like to understand how it is that most humans suffer from a lack of self-love, self-worth, and from not feeling valuable or needed. What I do know, though, is that we all experience one or all of these feelings at some point in our lives.

It is absolutely embarrassing for me to tell you how long it took me to get to the place of complete self-acceptance. Looking back, I don't believe my public face looked so insecure, but inside I was a frantic mess. Do you ever walk a street where there is a large crowd of people just passing by and wonder how people are feeling about themselves? Perhaps that's just me, but I wonder what's going on beneath the shell and the mask, beneath their high-powered, overconfident way that some people present themselves when you first meet them. I suppose it could be real. I suppose they could be that confident and that bold, but then as I watch longer, closer, and more deeply the inauthentic, scared, and intimidated parts do begin to surface.

I'm curious, what is that like for you? What is it like being in your skin, and what do you think could become possible if you finally, completely, and unequivocally without reservation accepted yourself exactly as you are? Imagine who you would be. Imagine what life would be like if you were flanked on both sides with friends and family all feeling authentic and honest and metaphorically naked, without any false faces or agendas. What could we be as a society if, instead of meeting each other wound to wound, we met each other from glorious self to glorious self?

As you might have recognized already, there is a certain amount of repetition throughout this invitation for you to return to your authentic self, and that is because there is so much interplay within paths that we walk as we are journeying home to ourselves. The redundancy in some ways is not something I can avoid because of this interplay.

My wish, want, hope, and dream for you is freedom. Free to be you, however you choose to present yourself.

I am a very proud grandmother. I'm not proud because my grandchildren are the most brilliant children walking on the face of the earth or the most talented; I'm proud simply because they bring so much joy into my life in the most unpretentious ways. Children, especially in my experience with grandchildren, are our constant reminder to love and accept ourselves as we are. When I'm with them and my three-year-old granddaughter decides to strip naked because she just wants to be naked, every cell in my body feels a certain amount of jealousy. That jealousy has everything to do with just wanting that level of freedom. I don't envy actors and actresses because so much of what they do seems pretend to me, but my grandchildren are just pure and wanting to be awake and alive and have fun, and when they walk into the room, they carry no baggage with them. I want more of that in my life, and I want that for my readers.

Can you imagine what it would feel like if we walked through our homes, in our jobs, and on our streets free of any pretense, carrying no weight of concern about how another individual sees us or measures us? Even as I pose the question here, I can feel the energetic shift in my body and I trust that as you use your imagination you, too, will experience this shift in your body. Our bodies never lie, so if our bodies enjoy this shift through our imagination this must be a worthy goal to set.

NOT BEING ME

I share this story with you with full permission from my ex-husband, as he and his wife, my husband, and I are great friends. We share holidays and vacations together. *(This is the beauty of waking up and healing.)*

My first marriage was the beginning of my inauthenticity. (You need to know that we are very close friends today and have spoken often of this dynamic. I say this because he is alive and will be reading this book, I'm sure.) While he is kind, wonderful, and very conscious, at the time of the beginning of our relationship he was very attracted to women who wore a lot of makeup and provocative clothes. That was not me: I was a natural, down-to-earth kind of girl, wearing khakis and T-shirts and no makeup. This did not seem to please him, and he would seemingly express in a variety of ways that it wasn't pleasing him. Sometimes, right before my eyes, he would stare at a woman who was the total opposite of me.

What did I do? I twisted myself into an inauthentic version of myself to get his approval. I was insecure and this seemed like the logical thing to do. But as you can imagine, I lost aspects of myself and did not retrieve those aspects for decades.

After our divorce, three things happened.

First, in my very next but temporary relationship with someone who definitely benefited from my insecurities, I had a third child. That relationship was created out of my inauthentic way of being. He didn't really want the parts of me that I hoped he would see; he wanted the parts of me that I had created to satisfy my soon-to-be ex-husband. Because this relationship was based on a lie that I was still maintaining, it crashed and burned in record time.

The second thing that happened is I became a minister. Being a minister caused me to stop and ponder a lot about my self-image and how I was to present myself to those under my care. Initially I dressed quite frumpy because I was afraid of conveying the wrong image in this new career of mine. I didn't really know how to present myself to the public. I wasn't even sure at this time what was an authentic look for me. I no longer enjoyed dressing like my grandmother, but when I modified my fashion choices, I was encouraged to cover up a bit and show less cleavage. (I never thought I was revealing too much.) Once again, you can see that I was still caught up in the habit of trying to please outside influences and I was not yet expressing myself authentically. I was not accepting myself as I was.

As time went on, I did finally find my balance and I discovered that I enjoy dressing with lots of color and flair—not fancy, just boldly. This was fun, this was me, and it would remain my way of dressing for my professional role going forward. You see, I was learning to love and accept myself as I am by my standards and no one else's. My focus changed and my consciousness shifted to one of self-acceptance, which led to living a more authentic life.

But the third and most wonderful thing that happened was that I met a man who loved me as I was. He didn't want me to be different in any way. However I showed up was fine with him. Whether dressed up or in sweats and flannel, he took me as me—and I married that man. What a relief it was to be loved and accepted as I was.

But let's be clear about the order of these changes. First, I changed how I felt about myself. I expanded my consciousness and emanated self-acceptance and then attracted a man who would reflect back to me an increased amount of self-love.

My first husband might have been the catalyst to my learning about myself, but he was not the cause. My self-doubt and lack of self-acceptance colored my consciousness and influenced my dance in this world. We are always living life from the inside out, whether we believe so or not. So I hold no ill will toward him, and besides that, he has changed and grown with self-awareness and is also happily married. People do not make you who you are. People do not make you feel what you are feeling. **You become who you are through how you feel about and measure yourself.** Those people are a mirror to how you feel and measure yourself.

To live an exceptionally authentic life we must first dive into the depths of our own being and seek the mental and emotional causes that we adopted through domestication.

To Thine Own Self Be True

The timeless wisdom of the phrase "To thine own self be true," spoken by Polonius in Shakespeare's Hamlet, *holds a profound truth that resonates deeply with the journey of spiritual authenticity. (Don't be too impressed: While I know the phrase, I had to research the source.) While it is often interpreted as advice to act in alignment with one's own values, it also invites us to delve deeper into the core of our being and discover the essence of who we truly are. This exploration of self is both a spiritual and practical journey, one that challenges us to strip away societal expectations, false narratives, and the limiting beliefs we've internalized over time.*

At its heart, being true to oneself requires an unrelenting commitment to authenticity. Authenticity, in this context, is not simply the act of "being yourself" as you are on the surface, but a journey toward uncovering and expressing your truest, most divine essence. It asks us to question: Who am I beyond the roles I play? What is the truth of my being when stripped of external validation or societal conditioning? This is the purpose of personal inquiry and contemplation.

There is a variety of interpretations about how authenticity demonstrates itself, and it is important to keep the highest expression of authenticity as your north star. Being true to your values is great, but if those values have been corrupted with your unhealed trauma, they may not be reflecting the highest possible expression of you. We are complicated beings; identifying your personal power by means of your authentic self takes effort and intention.

STRIP AWAY THE MASKS

Be yourself; everyone else is already taken.
—ATTRIBUTED TO OSCAR WILDE

Much of the challenge in being true to oneself lies in dismantling the masks we wear and the reasons we wear them. From an early age, many of us are conditioned to conform to societal norms or familial expectations. We become who we think we need to be to feel loved, accepted, or worthy. This is domestication in its fullest form. These masks serve as protection initially, but over time, they can distance us from our authentic self. I bet if you take a long, honest look at yourself you can identify some masks that you have come to believe as real.

While it is not the only place that we hide our inner self, the place where we find ourselves hiding the most is in our jobs. As a professional, standards are often laid out before us and your desire to be employed is one of the most tempting places for you to not be you. Blending in with the already established culture is what is expected, and your employment there takes priority over being your authentic self.

This might be one of the only times that choosing to wear a mask will work for you because it is like wearing a uniform. If your job had a uniform, you would wear it well; expressing a particular decorum in your job or profession is the same. But remember to take off that mask and that uniform as soon as you clock out. Playing in that world is not the same as becoming that world.

JOURNAL PROMPTS

Here are a few questions to help you look behind some of the masks that you might wear. Ask yourself:

- If I didn't need to be the smart, wise, funny one in the room all the time, who would I be?
- When I enter a room, what am I projecting to the current crowd to feel OK?
- As I work to love myself more, can I let go of the impressions I try to project to be accepted?
- What fear or insecurity is driving me to wear this _____ mask?
- How would my relationships change if I showed up as my authentic self?
- Am I acting out of alignment with my values to gain approval or avoid conflict?
- What aspects of myself do I hide because I fear they won't be accepted?
- Who am I when no one else is watching?

Ultimately, "to thine own self be true" is a call to be you, an undefended version of you. It is an invitation to live in alignment with our highest self, to embody the truth of who we are, and to honor the inner badass that you know you are. This commitment to authenticity is not a destination but a journey, one that unfolds moment by moment as we choose to live from a place of integrity, love, and truth.

Spiritual Mindshift Affirmation

It is with a sense of complete devotion to being the authentic expression of myself that I best embody the universal authenticity that exists at the heart of all of us. I am willing to be metaphorically naked, to strip away the masks that I have donned in order to navigate this life. I am willing to step out into the light, to be fully revealed without hesitation. I am willing to become a version of myself that I have never known before this moment. And while this may shake me to my core, I do it anyway.

The more authentic I am, the more courage I gain to express that authentic way of being. With deep and abundant gratitude, I surrender this word to the All That Is and allow it to become the guiding authority of my life.

And so it is.

POWER PRACTICES FOR SELF-ACCEPTANCE

- Everything you have read so far in this book hopefully has led you to being committed to who you are as you are. When you hear that negative small voice, the one that hovers in the back of your head, say anything that is unkind, say to yourself, out loud if possible, "STOP. This is not my truth."
- If you find yourself standing near someone who causes you to compare yourself, once again engage that self-empowering voice and say, "I am ENOUGH as I am."
- If you are tempted to regret some life choices, refocus your attention and say, "I accept what is and bless all that has brought me here."
- Consider using this affirmation as a mantra or create your own. If you create your own, make sure it is incredibly uplifting. "I accept myself as I am and as I am not."

DANCE WITH ME IN YOUR IMAGINATION

Begin to imagine your world and all the paths you walk—each step a moment to savor. Picture walking alongside others who also love and accept themselves, and how effortless and joyful that path could be. Imagine bringing with you the people you love—your friends, your family, and your children, encouraging them to embrace themselves just as they are.

Now, imagine the atmosphere. Imagine breathing air that is free of self-judgment and harsh criticism. How light, how free, how joy-filled you might feel in such a space.

Envision a world where everyone loves themselves unconditionally—and from that deep well of self-love, we come together, creating a world shaped by mutual respect, compassion, and authenticity.

JOURNAL PROMPTS

Write freely in your journal without editing or judging what you write. The freer you are with yourself, the more the wisdom will rise through you.

- Make a list of your unique qualities and express appreciation for them.
- Become conscious about the parts of you that you have criticized and write a letter to those parts apologizing for criticizing them.
- What activities, passions, or quirks once brought you joy but got buried under self-doubt, responsibility, or fear? Now invite them back into your life.

* Write a love letter to a part of yourself that you've neglected or silenced.
* If you fully accept every part of yourself—flaws, quirks, and all—how would you show up differently in your life?
* How would your legacy be different if you choose to accept yourself completely? What would you be modeling?
* Close your eyes, take a deep breath, and listen inward. What part of you is quietly asking to be seen, heard, or nurtured today, and write from that place.

A SPIRITUAL MINDSHIFT TO UPLEVEL YOUR SELF-ACCEPTANCE

I throw my hands up in complete surrender and allow myself and my attention to take in all the surrounding beauty, both in the obvious and not-so-obvious places. I am moved and inspired to have a new idea about myself. I am moved to know myself in the most intimate way that I have ever known myself before. Right now, on this day, I choose to accept myself exactly as I am and as I am not.

I choose to move into a habit of self-acceptance that is forever evolving, where I am always finding newer and more expanded ways to accept and love myself. This evolution inside me is a form of self-love. It is grand to accept all aspects of myself without reservation, limitation, or hesitation. I declare, going forth, that I accept and love myself like never before in my life.

A LOVE LETTER TO MYSELF

Dearest Self,

Today, I celebrate you for walking the brave and beautiful path of self-acceptance. This is the path where judgment loosens its grip and truth becomes your resting place. There is no greater power in an individual than one who accepts themselves as they are.

You have stopped waiting to be different to be worthy. You no longer withhold love from yourself until you've changed, improved, or arrived. Instead, you've begun to welcome yourself, as you are, in this moment—with open arms.

You've learned to embrace your whole self: the light and the shadow, the flaws and the brilliance, the parts still healing and the ones already whole. You've realized that self-acceptance is not resignation, it's recognition. It's saying yes to who you are while still allowing space to grow.

There is such peace in your presence now. Such relief in no longer needing to perform, explain, or edit yourself to feel like enough.

I honor you for this sacred journey inward. May you continue to see yourself clearly and hold yourself lovingly. You are worthy of belonging—to yourself—every day, exactly as you are.

With unwavering love,
Me

REMEMBER TO BREATHE

For this practice, I am encouraging you to combine your conscious, mindful breath with your spoken word. As always, you might want to be alone; however, if you are a parent, consider doing this in front of your kids.

Stand up, open your arms, take a deep breath, and affirm "I accept myself as I am and I love me this way," and exhale. Be bold and enjoy the practice.

Let's Conclude with These Affirmations

- I give myself permission to accept myself exactly as I am—and exactly as I am not.
- I am enough, always and already.
- I am the place where love resides.
- **I demand to be me—without excuses.**

PEARLS OF WISDOM

At this point in the book, I get teary as I ask you to accept yourself as you are. I'm teary because I know how difficult it is to love and accept yourself, and to have that self-compassion we spoke about in the last chapter, because most of us were not reared or educated in this aspect of the self. It pains me greatly when I see people who beat themselves up who have no sense of their self-worth, who have no belief that they deserve to accept themselves exactly as they are. So the pearl of wisdom from this chapter is to not wait or to think you have to prove it but to begin to accept yourself, all of yourself, every bit that ever was or ever will be, and to do so now and to do so boldly. To be the one who truly dances like nobody's watching.

9

WALKING IN THE UNSHAKABLE KNOWING OF WHO YOU ARE

The Path of Self-Confidence

It is revolutionary for any trans person to choose to be seen and visible in a world that tells us we should not exist.

—LAVERNE COX

DESCRIPTION OF SELF-CONFIDENCE

Self-confidence is the energetic key to moving through the world while believing in one's own gifts and talents, and trusting that their self-confidence will be communicated both silently and through their accomplishments.

HERE IS A QUICK START OPTION

When self-doubt creeps in, even a little, stop entertaining that inner chatter and say to yourself, "I am a spiritual badass, ready to be in the world in a powerful way." (Do this with no hesitation whatsoever.) And remember to walk confidently, stand up straight, pull those shoulders back, hold your head high, and be in the world like you belong there and you know it.

I have included self-confidence in this book because self-confidence is a necessary part of the formula for a life well lived. Please be ready to be radically honest with yourself not only along this path but also through all the aspects of your journey. Don't confuse self-confidence with arrogance; it is totally different. It has nothing to do with being conceited or self-serving, and I will build a strong case for that.

You were born with a divine birthright for joy, peace, health, wealth, and happiness, but often your adoptive ways close you down so early. That birthright was created by universal intelligence, that which created you, and all that is, and it creates through us along with our conscious participation. If this is not your belief, maybe you can suspend any objections for just a little while and see if what I have to say might just work for you.

You might see yourself as part of a spiritual network, or maybe you believe in an outside God, the all-supreme being that created you. Either way, we are still talking about a power that creates. That which created you also creates through you. To the degree that you love, honor, and accept yourself, you will have greater access to this universal power. That power—call it God, Spirit, Intelligence, One, Love, or something else—is an infinite flow of creative energy seeking to express itself in the most beautiful and amazing ways. Those who walk confidently stride in this knowing.

Your confidence is not about your human self; your confidence is about recognizing that which formed you, because it informs you and your way of being, and it is a consistent cause in and through your life.

This One of which I speak expresses at the heart of you because you can never be separate from that which created you, just as you cannot separate two sides of a coin. The cells of your grandmother lived inside your mother; and when you were born, some of those cells and the cells of your mother were born with you. In the same way that you will always be part of your birth lineage, you will always be part of that powerful spark that gave life when the egg and the sperm came together.

Yes, when that egg and sperm came together, a divine spark exploded and the blueprint that created you began. It is nothing less than a miracle that you are here, so for you to not celebrate your life every day is a huge mistake. You are worthy of celebration.

Science contains the explanation for you being you, and if you apply this reasoning to who you are and how you were created, you have a choice in how you express yourself. Your confidence is not the result of your skills and talents; your skills and talents are the result of your confidence. It is a mistake to believe that you must become better at something before you can feel and express confidence.

When you become really good at a skill, that should not be the beginning of your confidence but a reminder of how worthy you are to be in this dance of life and to dance boldly.

The truth is this: Confidence is born from connection. When you become intimately connected to your source—whatever that may be—you allow confidence to grow naturally from that relationship. Honor and praise the power that created you, and that power will expand as it moves through you.

Even if you view yourself purely as the result of biological forces and scientific processes, the principle remains the same: Science explains the mechanics of your existence, but the energy that formed you is still at work within you. Whether you call it Spirit, Source, or the brilliance of nature, it flows through you—shaping you and expressing itself as you. Confidence isn't something you chase; it's something you allow.

My family heritage is English and Irish, but primarily English. Being English meant manners and decorum and so at a young age I was sent to a set of classes that would teach me how to walk confidently into a room, how to carry myself, how to sit—with my legs crossed—properly of course, and how to eat in public. It was called *charm school.* Just for your amusement I will tell you that this whole thing was a total farce because within the walls of my home I was existing in a totally dysfunctional family atmosphere.

This training worked for the public view of things, allowed me to walk into a room looking confident with my head held high, my shoulders back, my stomach in, and as I entered any room or restaurant your opinion of me would have been based on my learned but very inauthentic behavior. There's no mystery why being authentic matters so much to me.

I presented well, I looked confident, I behaved according to social norms, but inside, it was a totally different story.

Those lessons paid off and made my parents look great, but inside I was a total mess, a disaster. My posture only accomplished one thing: intimidating other girls and women. I might have looked confident, but it was all a lie. Some of you reading this know this experience. Over the years, when given the opportunity to share my truth, some are shocked, and yet others get it. I have become so sensitive to how a lack of confidence displays itself that I often feel brokenhearted for those in my classes or coaching program.

When I recognize this lack of confidence, I just want to crawl inside the skin of another and show them how to be, how to stand, how to walk in a room and how to believe in themselves. A lack of self-confidence leaves its mark in so many ways, and it is always unbecoming.

It is this lack of confidence that will unfortunately attract a bully or a dominant partner or an overbearing boss into your life. Our behavior and our silent communication attracts us to the opposite personal traits as a silent and unspoken effort to heal that part. This is our shadow at work. (For more on shadows, see my book *Shadow Work: A Spiritual Path to Healing and Integration.*)

A lack of self-confidence is widespread among our daughters and it is deeply influenced by social media, unconscious bias, and a long-standing culture shaped by white supremacy. These dynamics don't exist in isolation—they are energetically entangled. Where timidity shows up, you'll often find an overbearing personality nearby. Where confidence is lacking, someone who thrives on intimidation is usually close at hand.

Let's also stay aware of the shadow side of confidence. In this book we are focusing on the "light" side of confidence communicated through one who knows themselves well, but there is a shadow side to this as well (as with everything), and this shadow side shows up as a gross overcompensation for not feeling confident. Some individuals mask their insecurities by a false projection of confidence, which can be read by others as arrogance. And the reason for that is when it is not authentic, it is adopted, and an adopted confidence looks like arrogance. This is an attempt to shape one's self-worth. You can recognize the difference by how fragile you might feel when being in public.

Here is what authentic self-confidence silently communicates: Self-confidence says that you are fully and completely aware of and connected to the glorious power that created you. With every breath you are aware of the stunning intelligence coming through you. When you walk into a room, you are never alone, you are walking with the power that created you along with the wisdom of your ancestors.

When you stand tall, you are silently displaying your potent connection to the network of life that flows through you. You are quietly connected to all that exists, just as the mycelium that runs beneath our feet connects all of Mother Earth to everything else, feeding nature with life-nurturing elements.

In this way, your confidence never needs to be dependent on your skills, talents, or education. Your confidence is sourced from your conscious awareness of your connection to all of life. As you call forth your confidence, all the skills, talents, and education you have will expand and you will access it with more ease. As you continue to call in to your experience greater confidence, you will find yourself gathering new inner resources that were there all the time.

Take your desire to grow in confidence and combine it with a commitment to silent meditation—deep and extended periods of stillness—and you will begin to unearth profound insight from within. Understanding about a variety of things will begin to emerge, almost as if by magic. I know it may sound like a fairy tale, but we must remember genius is available to all who listen deeply.

My own devotion to silent meditation has granted me a wealth of wisdom and clarity. When paired with my growing self-confidence, it has positioned me to serve as a teacher, coach, and author—empowered to support others in learning to love themselves more fully.

Underneath all your self-denigrating habits lives a bold and powerfully confident you. This is your authentic self. As you learn that your confidence cannot be measured by accomplishments alone but is measured by your universal connections, your authentic self will come into greater expressiveness. You deserve to know yourself in this way, beloved. You deserve the full force of the creative process surging through you as your authentic self, totally free to dance like no one is watching.

FEELING LIKE A FAKE / THE IMPOSTOR SYNDROME

When we live authentically, there is no need to fear being found out because we are not performing or saving face—we are being our fully expressed self.

No book on authenticity would be complete without looking at the classic and well-worn impostor syndrome. Healing this syndrome is going to make a huge difference in your life. Impostor syndrome is the echo of our domesticated self that was never affirmed. We are here to learn that we do not have to earn our self-confidence, self-worth, or self-love; we simply need to accept it.

Let me try to describe what this syndrome is and how it shows itself in simple language.

As a coach and spiritual counselor, I constantly run into this experience with my clients. And I, too, know this experience intimately. The impostor syndrome is the name of the experience given to individuals who lack the confidence of their opinions, level of education, or experience as they seek to express themselves in the world. It is an indicator of a serious lack of confidence in oneself to the point that even with a measure of success, they still feel like frauds.

This syndrome is deep-seated and not easy to recognize without focused introspection and support of an expert, because the feeling that accompanies this experience is a lack of confidence that causes the individual to hide, play small, and not stand out even when they are quite accomplished in their expertise. This experience can exist concurrently in someone who is a known expert, because impostor syndrome is not about their education or their experience; it is sourced from a sad, scared inner child.

This experience will be more prevalent in one who has not journeyed down the road of shadow work. It's quite fascinating just how easily this syndrome can hide right in front of us.

JOURNAL PROMPTS

Here are some prompts to jar your thinking and to help you find out if you have known these experiences:

- When have you felt like a fraud, even while succeeding?
- What parts of you have you hidden because you claimed them as not good enough?
- While you might feel like an impostor, how do you think others see you or think of you?
- If you could finally feel like you are enough, how might you show up differently?

Let's look at a few ways that this syndrome might show up.

- When given a compliment, you might say something like: "It was nothing," but in truth it was the result of a huge effort. This response is a way of hiding your lack of confidence and how uncomfortable you are with being celebrated. Experiencing impostor syndrome leads to the habit of shrinking yourself and hiding your light.
- This happens because you have forgotten your divine essence, your brilliance. It's possible that you are confusing humility with self-denial due to your discomfort. Maybe someone told you not to be so full of yourself or warned you from being too arrogant or conceited.
- Try using the following affirmation to counter this tendency: "I no longer shrink to fit in. I honor who I am and all my gifts. I am potent and willing to be seen as such."
- Another way this shows up is through the self-imposed pressure

to prove oneself. Oh man, I really wish I did not know this experience personally, but alas, I did and I still do at times, especially through my many years as a minister and teacher.

- The overdoer is so commonplace in our society that we often applaud those who do too much—you know, the overachiever. We love overachievers and we love being an overachiever until we exhaust ourselves mentally and emotionally. We often take pride in our exhaustion.
- There might come a time when you just can't do one more thing, and this is where your fear of being found out as an impostor or a fraud appears right in front of you. Be careful here. Shame can kick in very quickly.
- Maybe you know someone or maybe this is true for you to have a need to overdo, overperform, or have a very full plate in an effort to get others' approval and hide the sense that you are not enough. Sound familiar by any chance? Are you looking for applause and accolades even while losing yourself in this cycle of thinking?
- Try using the following affirmation to counter this tendency: "I no longer need to go above and beyond to prove what is already true about me: I am perfect the way I am."
- For many individuals who live under this syndrome, they exist with the constant fear of being found out. Those are individuals who discount their current intelligence, intuition, and accomplishments so completely they don't allow them to be counted for with any amount of confidence or self-satisfaction. Often, this person thinks, *I'm not as good as they think*. They brace themselves for failure and collapse—all while things are actually working.
- It's truly quite fascinating that this feeling can coexist with all evidence to the contrary. This fear arises when your soul forgets that it is rooted in truth, in the Divine.
- Try using the following affirmation to counter this tendency:

"I am not an impostor. I am an instrument of the Divine and I am evidence of brilliance."

* This next sign is one that I know intimately, and I will share a personal story with you below. It's a story to demonstrate the danger of not accepting the invitation to be fully expressed.
* When we distance ourselves from spirit-ordained opportunities, there are times that we are so fearful of failing in the face of opportunity that we don't make room for the opportunity at all. We shrink away, deny what's possible, and unconsciously refuse to embrace the gifts that have been offered.
* Not unlike the other shades of feeling like an impostor, this is rooted in your belief that you are not enough. Not being enough is a global epidemic, as it hides in plain sight.
* Try using the following affirmation to counter this tendency: "I claim, declare, and call forth my readiness to be seen and celebrated. I say *yes* to all the glorious opportunities being offered."

Saying *Yes* to Spirit's Push

About thirty years ago at the beginning of my journey to be licensed as a minister, I regularly attended wonderful meditation retreats that were populated with equally dedicated individuals. The meditations were silent and very long. Throughout the silence, a musician who was present would strike a single note on the piano. The purpose of this was to keep people awake and plugged into the silence—in other words, no sleeping.

This was what happened during one of our long meditations: The next time a note was struck on the piano, I did not just hear the note—I felt it. Yes, I felt it vibrate through me. And the next time the teacher spoke, as he picked up the microphone to say something, once again I felt the movement of his lips before he spoke and as he spoke.

I admit to you that this scared me to a certain degree. I couldn't figure out what was happening. Suddenly I was not only listening, but I was also experiencing every sound in the room. This hearing-

and-feeling sensation continues to this day. When a plane flies overhead, I feel it down my spine as much as I hear it.

Here is the point of my sharing this story. During Q&A at the retreat, I nervously shared my experience. The teacher, who already knew that I was journeying the path of ministry, said to me, "How do you expect to be a minister if you can't feel the room?" While I wasn't sure what to make of his response initially, I knew intuitively that this was a critical moment along my life's journey and felt this was a gift being offered to me.

I had two separate, powerful reactions. My first was fear. It felt scary to be feeling all these things I was feeling. My second reaction was the most important one.

I knew that I had to say yes to the offering. I knew that this gift required that I consciously say yes and accept its reality in my life. So, while all charged up with emotion, I found my way to a staircase where I could be alone and stated out loud to God, "Yes. I say yes. I am willing to accept this as a gift." To this day I am grateful for knowing deeply within myself that to receive a gift is not to be frightened of it.

Claiming your skills, talents, and beauty must be celebrated and accepted if you want to have access to them.

And lastly, there are the perfectionists. Perfectionists are convinced that they must do more, do better, do the best, and be the best, and anything to the contrary is frightening to them.

Perfectionists feel compelled to do things perfectly but without knowing why or without feeling satisfied once they have accomplished it. It is never enough. They will often delay sharing their work or speaking about themselves in an affirming way even in the light of great accomplishment. It is sad, really, because this is all about self-denial.

Perfection is like a mask, a costume worn to feel safe. What's sad is that behind their mask they are hiding their brilliance, which is possible to show when they step into their authenticity.

Try using the following affirmation to counter this tendency:

"I consciously release any tendency to judge myself and my work as not good enough, and I choose to show up as I am, ready to stand in my authenticity and power."

HOW DO WE STOP LIVING WITH IMPOSTOR SYNDROME?

1. We begin by naming the experience so we can recognize it when it shows up. Remember, awareness is the initial key for transformation.
2. Identify the voices that add to your hiding. Acknowledge messages from family, teachers, and friends. Have you been guilty of trying to live up to others, or to social media?
3. Recognize and reclaim your truth by calling out this behavior and using affirmations or other spiritual practices to create change.
4. Become a model of transformation as you encourage others to do the same work. This will immediately reinforce your journey and is especially important if you are a parent or a teacher. Learn how to invite those under your influence to value themselves for who they are naturally.

POWER PRACTICES FOR SELF-CONFIDENCE

- ✶ STOP questioning yourself. Trust yourself. Trust your opinions.
- ✶ Stop apologizing for simple and silly things. Yes, of course apologize if you said or did something truly offensive, but beyond that, just stop.
- ✶ Affirm yourself all day, every day.
- ✶ As silly as this always seems, look in the mirror and say, "I love you and I believe in you."
- ✶ Take chances, take risks, raise your hand, and choose to be counted.

DANCE WITH ME IN YOUR IMAGINATION

Imagine walking confidently in your own footsteps, feeling the full measure and power of the universe supporting you. Picture your ancestors lifting you up, encouraging you to embrace the fullness of your being.

Now imagine carrying an air of confidence that opens doors and creates opportunities—one that allows you to model a new way of being for your lineage and your legacy.

And finally, imagine walking shoulder to shoulder with a community of people—with no one needing to outshine or outproduce another. Just shared dignity, mutual respect, and the quiet peace that comes from knowing we are enough, together.

JOURNAL PROMPTS

Write freely in your journal without editing or judging what you write. The freer you are with yourself, the more the wisdom will rise through you. Ask yourself:

- What distracts me the most from being me?
- Who do I compare myself to and why?
- When do I find myself wishing I was more confident?
- What would my life be like if I walked in confidence?
- What hero/shero would I most like to emulate who *seems* to have great confidence?
- Finish this sentence: I walk confidently into any room because I know . . .

A SPIRITUAL MINDSHIFT TO UPLEVEL YOUR SELF-CONFIDENCE

I speak this word for myself today in the most holy and stunning way possible. I take off the gloves and confidently begin to recognize myself as a fully realized and fully orbed human being in all ways that matter. I am confident in my intelligence, in my ability to love, in my ability to heal, and in my creative self-expression. I am confident that I am a worthy human, bringing love, acceptance, and compassion to the world. Wherever I go, I bring the best of me along. Whoever I engage with, I engage with complete confidence that all communication is clean, open, authentic, and real.

I now consciously accept the growth of my confidence in all areas of my life, based not on accomplishments but on my inner relationship with the Divine, and it is so beautiful.

And so it is!

A LOVE LETTER TO MYSELF

Dearest Self,

Today, I honor the strength and steadiness you've found on the path of self-confidence. What a journey it has been—learning to trust your voice, your choices, and your presence in the world.

There was a time when you doubted your worth, when you questioned your abilities, when you looked outside yourself for permission to shine. But those days are fading. You've begun to remember who you are. And it is happening now—boldly, brilliantly.

You now walk with more certainty. You speak with more clarity. You stand tall, not because you have all the answers, but because you've learned to trust the wisdom within. You've stopped measuring yourself by comparison and started measuring by your truth, your innate worth.

Each time you take a step forward, despite fear or uncertainty, you build a foundation of inner trust. That's what confidence truly is—not arrogance or bravado, but the quiet knowing that you are capable, valuable, and enough.

I celebrate the way you now carry yourself—with grace, power, and self-respect. May your confidence continue to rise from within, rooted in your authenticity and your undeniable light.

With belief and deep pride,
Me

REMEMBER TO BREATHE

Every time you look in the mirror, look deeply in your eyes, take a nice, full, deep breath and, upon the exhalation breath, say, "Yes, I am wonderfully alive."

Let's Conclude with These Affirmations

- I now give myself permission to walk boldly, speak freely, and stand fully in my power.
- I trust my voice, my path, and my worth.
- I am a bold, brilliant, and confident being.
- **I demand to be me—without excuses.**

PEARLS OF WISDOM

Self-confidence is such a juicy conversation, and I hope that you have received enough support from this chapter to realize that self-confidence is something to claim and declare, not after you've done something right, but beforehand. When you claim self-confidence without a reason, the reason comes. Confidence is about walking in the light, love, and power of the intelligence of this universe. So when you say, "I am confident, I live in this confidence, I walk in this confidence, and I act from this confidence," your confidence and the paths through your life multiply, especially as you return to your authenticity, getting wider and brighter and more beautiful. Walk confidently, my friend, my dear reader, not because you happened to do something right, but because you deserve the confidence of spirit in you.

10

REMEMBER, YOU WERE NEVER BROKEN

The Path of Self-Worth

Raise your words, not voice. It is rain that grows flowers, not thunder.
—ATTRIBUTED TO RUMI

Description of Self-Worth

Self-worth is the awareness that you are worthy of all good and great expression, even if you can't explain why. It is a deep and profound belief that you are a child of the Beloved One and deserve to live a fully expressed life—without explaining yourself.

Here Is a Quick Start Option

There is only one way to begin raising your self-worth, and that is through diligent and mindful awareness of your thoughts. Then have at the ready a mantra or affirmation that you can use to counter the impact of negative self-talk. In other words, nip it in the bud—each and every time.

All metaphysical teachers, coaches, therapists, and counselors are no strangers to the lack of self-worth and how it universally connects people. The only word I can use to describe my experience as a teacher who is constantly engaging with people who are lacking in self-worth is *sad*. It is sad how all-consuming the feeling of low self-worth is, and it is difficult to identify the source of this issue. A lack of self-worth is born from a variety of subtle places within ourselves.

When teaching any of the courses that I have taught for decades, I often tear up when I recognize once *again* one of my students doubting their self-worth. I wish this was a rare event, but unfortunately it is common beyond understanding or explanation.

Low self-worth is a major factor contributing to poor relationships, lack of success, and low self-confidence and self-love. It can also be considered a risk factor in criminal behavior, while it may not be a sole or direct cause.

When our lack of self-worth remains unchallenged, it causes us to view the world through a lens that reflects the darkest version of ourselves. It can leave us so blind that we become convinced of its reality while lacking any true understanding of it. Unearthing our lack of self-worth may be one of the most painful aspects of the personal journey while being one of the most important. It lives at the heart of everything you are attempting to do.

As we begin to take inventory of our lives, if we remain unaware, the resulting frustration and confusion can take our very breath away. It rears its nasty head just as we begin to reach for the life of our dreams. The higher we dream and reach, the more it attempts to sabotage us. It lurks in our subconscious like a computer virus, quietly undermining our efforts to become a fully expressed version of ourselves.

And here is a very high truth to learn and remember: **You cannot create yourself outside of what you believe yourself to be, and if you do not believe yourself to be worthy, it will leave its mark everywhere.** You are what you believe about yourself. This belief in a lack of self-worth will undermine you at every step you take to free yourself from its conditioning. You're probably wondering how to free yourself from this intense but silent killer of your soul:

1. The first step is to acknowledge its presence and then begin to explore its origins—though some of its roots may remain hidden.

Low self-worth is often a silent thief of joy and potential. While I will outline a few of its possible sources, I encourage you not to use them as fuel for blame or resentment. Instead, see them as opportunities for understanding and healing.

Some potential psychological causes are:

* **Childhood trauma or abuse.** Experiences of any kind of abuse often lead the one suffering from it to believe they are the cause. A sense of shame and a lack of self-worth is often the result leading to this persistent and painful experience.
* **Parental influence (or rather a lack of skillful parenting).** Whether it was a lack of attention—unintentional as it may have been, perhaps due to the need to work and provide—or the result of a poor self-image they carried into their role as a parent, the impact was still felt.
* **Bullying or social rejection.** If you were different in any way, children can be cruel, so if you were bullied or harassed, the ensuing social exclusion or adopting shame can follow you into your adulthood.
* **A sense of inadequacy.** If left unchallenged, inadequacy can live at the heart of your lack of self-worth. If you struggled in school because you were a late bloomer or had a developmental assessment, for example, that time of struggle may have been an opportunity for your increased self-judgment. Unfortunately, many schools in the United States are not set up to redirect your attention that would have allowed you to be patient as you caught up with your peers.
* **Mental health issues.** Whether or not they were diagnosed, mental health challenges had a direct impact upon your sense of self. In addition, if your parents had any kind of mental health or substance abuse issues, they—being your main models—would have left their marks.

Intelligence and pure potential, as wonderful as they are, can be easily minimized and undermined when you do not believe in yourself. Self-worth and self-approval are the influences that free your intellect, potential, and creativity to be expressed; otherwise they sit unharvested, and the fruit of your brilliance will die on the vine, rot, and become toxic. It is critical for your mental and physical health that you believe in yourself and be generous in your self-discovery.

2. Once you raise your self-awareness about the potential sources of your lack of self-worth, next you must make the decision to challenge your unjustified tendency to believe it. Yes, you must make a new habit of challenging all thoughts and feelings that feed that belief. Every thought becomes part of our reality unless we pull them up like weeds in a garden out of the inner landscape of our consciousness.

   This can be as simple as saying *no* when feelings or thoughts arise, or you can have a mantra or affirmation at the ready. Create something short and easy to remember and repeat, and don't for a moment negate the value of hanging a reminder around your living space.

Waking Up Happy

As a young adult, beginning to have a family, I carried into this time of my life a measure of personal trauma that had not been properly addressed. As a girl, I had to constantly protect myself from my father. Most mornings if he came to wake me for school, I can remember feeling braced and protective because I didn't trust his intentions.

Years later, as a wife and mother, my mornings were filled with waking up kind of angry for no reason. Upon some contemplation, I came to realize that my anger was a carryover from my past and not rooted in my current life with my husband and my boys.

This is how I decided to handle it. At the time, we slept in a canopy bed, so I chose to write a note to myself and hang it right over my head so I would see it upon awakening. The note said, "It's OK to wake up happy." Did it change overnight? No, of course not, but over

> *time it did work. I had to reprogram my thinking and my reactions to my world. I'm grateful to tell you that I began to feel safe.*
>
> *When we are* changing our minds, *it takes some effort to do so thoroughly.*

Set some personal reminders for yourself or try one of these affirmations:

* I am worthy of all good—all the time.
* I was born worthy of a well-lived life, and I live that life now.
* My essence is beautiful and strong, and I am worthy of celebration.

3. The next concept is borrowed from the Twelve Steps of Alcoholics Anonymous—fake it until you make it. Believe it until you achieve it. Walk around pretending to know your worth, act like it, speak like it, and make decisions based on believing in yourself until you finally, totally believe it. Sounds a tad crazy, but it works. You want to practice it until it works itself into your system completely, until it is part of how you see and sense yourself.

Let me repeat myself: You are a beautiful reflection of the Divine. I believe in you. I believe in your fullest expression and know that you are worthy of all good—all the time.

This is how we must speak to ourselves. I have watched many an individual in my years of teaching alter their self-talk, and it is amazing how their world shifts and changes accordingly. When we finally take to prioritizing our inner conversation, our self-talk, our world begins to shift, which of course is why it is included as part of our path to return to our authentic self. Oh, I can recall how unkind I was in my own mind before I chose to dedicate myself to growing and healing from the world I adopted in the most unconscious ways.

Before my dedication to these changes, I often referred to myself as weak, poor, inept, uneducated, and extremely needy. I was constantly looking for a way to feel full and loved because I couldn't get in touch with my own resources. You, me, all of us, deserve to float through life on a ribbon of beauty, strength, and love.

I know I'm being redundant here—I've said this before in this book—but I'll say it again: You are not at the mercy of what was. Not now. Not ever. You are not even at the mercy of what you've believed about yourself.

Why do I repeat this so often? Because rewiring your brain takes time. It takes deliberate effort to retrain your thoughts and rewire your synapses to the point where who you choose to be—and how you choose to see yourself—becomes automatic.

THE "OTHER" SELVES WE MUST FACE

As we dance the path toward authenticity, it's important to pause and acknowledge the quieter voices within—the ones that do not always uplift us but have shaped our inner world, nonetheless. We all have them but not everyone is listening for them. This might be a new skill you are developing; this self-awareness muscle needs your practice to activate it and your attention to grow.

These parts often hide in our shadow: the voices of self-condemnation, self-doubt, self-criticism, and self-denial. They stay hidden because they are subtle and we have normalized them.

I bring your attention back to these voices not because I want to linger on them but because I know how sneaky and insidious they are, and because much of that inner voice is not yours, it is the voice of the collective sneaking in through your subconscious. Your subconscious is never asleep; it notes everything, and many of these messages promote doubt and fear. Your subconscious sees everything from billboard advertisements and news headlines to social media posts. Your subconscious hears everything also, even when you are not paying attention—especially when you are not paying attention. This is why this work is a lifelong journey.

For decades I have attempted to teach my sons, and all my students, to *never, ever* watch television unless you are holding the remote in your hand

and can mute the commercials. I don't really care about commercials making you want possessions, but I care deeply about you unconsciously listening to commercials that plant seeds into your subconscious about illness, not being skinny enough, not being young-looking enough, not smelling good enough, and so on. Advertising often plays on our insecurities and fears, and can make them even worse. Why, you ask? Because when you are not paying attention—especially when you are not paying attention—those messages get in and can add negativity to your life. By editing out commercials, you are taking conscious steps toward setting some boundaries about negative messaging.

On the spiritual path we often call the conscious mind the *gatekeeper*, but to benefit from it, you are required to pay attention. It is time to wake up and realize that the world we live in, the world of commercialism that has been created of the collective greed of the 2 percent, impacts the whole. This is not about implying that making money or having things is a negative thing; this is about not falling asleep to become a willing target for the marketing giants whose only goal is to feed their bottom line without caring about how it impacts you personally.

It is important to remember that these inner voices are not enemies, though they often feel like obstacles. They were formed in response to something—perhaps harsh words spoken to us in childhood, a culture that told us we weren't enough, or painful moments that led us to believe we needed to become someone else to be loved. These inner voices created by our ego learned to protect us, even as they constrained us. They built armor around your heart, telling you not to shine too brightly, not to speak too boldly, not to be too much, but it was with a sense of protection that they were created. This is another reminder that all of life is for us—and sometimes we have to look a bit closer.

As you raise your self-awareness, these other voices can be looked at as either blocks that separate you from your inner strength or as stepping stones that lead you along the path of self-realization. This is what I teach in my course that correlates with this book on authenticity. The people in your life and the messages that you begin to uncover are in fact a blessing—yes, a blessing.

The people in your life who irritate you are there to point out your growth edge. The feelings of inadequacy might get sparked by others, but their purpose is to hold a mirror up to you so you can set yourself on a personal trajectory toward your spiritual and emotional emancipation.

A Story About a Donkey

This farmer had a donkey, and one day when the donkey wandered off, he fell into a hole that was too deep to climb out of. The farmer was very distressed but without a solution, feeling defeated, he decided to bury the donkey in the hole right where he was rather than have him starve in there.

He went home to retrieve a shovel and, feeling very dismayed, began throwing a shovelful of dirt at a time on top of the donkey. But the donkey had a very different idea because every time the farmer threw a shovel of dirt on top of the donkey, he simply shook his head to let it fall to the ground and stepped on top of it. The farmer, realizing that he was actually saving the donkey, worked faster. With each shovelful of dirt, the donkey climbed one step at a time until he was able to step out of the hole.

The moral of story: Don't claim defeat too early; see past the illusion of blocks to the solution of stepping stones to climb right out of your situation.

There are "other selves" we want to pay attention to; and to do so, you must develop a deep listening. Many of these messages have been normalized in our society:

* Self-condemnation whispers, "Who do you think you are?"
* Self-doubt answers, "You probably can't do it anyway."
* Self-criticism chimes in, "You should've known better."
* Self-denial shrinks us down, saying, "It's safer not to need, not to feel, not to want."

And yet, none of these quiet aspects are the truth of who you are. They are echoes—learned, inherited, and absorbed. They are survival strategies, not soul expressions. Simply said, they are lies that caught our attention when we weren't watching or didn't have the skill to determine their negative impact. But the you who is reading this book is clearly ready to recognize them, challenge them, and free yourself from such influences.

To live authentically, we must lovingly recognize these voices, not banish them but integrate them and welcome them home like your inner child who wants to be seen, welcomed, and loved. We must meet them with the healing forces contained within that are powerful enough to transmute their energy. Those forces are self-love, self-compassion, self-acceptance, and self-worth. As we fire up the heat under these affirming aspects, the self-limiting ideas will melt away. Your strength of focus will do that for you.

Self-compassion and the other healing forces do not shame the critical voices; they soften them. They don't argue with doubt; they hold it tenderly until it feels safe enough to transform. Self-compassion says, "I see you. I know you've been hurt, but you don't have to guard me anymore. I choose love now."

This kind of compassion isn't a onetime event. It's a daily practice. It's choosing, again and again, to treat yourself the way you might treat a dear friend—with kindness, patience, curiosity, and grace. As you do, something profound happens: Those old voices begin to lose their influence. And in their place, your authentic self—your whole, radiant, sacred self—begins to rise.

So, as you walk this path, bring all of you along. Don't leave the fearful voices behind; bring them into the light. Let them be seen. And then, gently, remind them of the deeper truths:

- You are not your self-doubt.
- You are not your self-condemnation.
- You are not your self-denial.
- You are the very essence of Life, God, and Spirit itself.

* You are the one who notices, the one who chooses, the one who loves. And that is where your freedom begins, but first you must remember to be in choice as you take responsibility for the redirection.

And, at the risk of beating the proverbial drum, be ready to consistently nip those limiting messages in the bud over and over again. It will take some time to reclaim some of the power that leaked out because you believed those voices, but hang in there. I have said it before: Remember to have a powerful statement in your pocket ready to be pulled out and used each and every time you catch one of those erroneous messages.

It can be as simple as: This is not my truth. I am more than this message. I deny this message. Or you can repeat the classic by Raymond Charles Barker: There isn't a word of truth in it. Over dedicated time, the limiting messages will be usurped by your chosen ones.

Not to brag, but I have to be honest; I am a bit of an overachiever when it comes to conditioning my mind. I don't let these unwanted, limiting thoughts hang out any longer than the time it takes for me to notice them. When people initially come along this path of watching their mind to catch what is conditioning them, it is a tad crazymaking at first, but it gets easier and quicker with practice.

The rewards are so worth it. Let me share with you some of the rewards I enjoy. I have ceased criticizing myself. I believe that I live with a vast amount of potentiality and the right to achieve my goals. I care for myself in ways I never did before. My relationships are now a reflection of my self-love and self-acceptance, which is what happens whenever you raise your self-love quotient.

Life is meant to be enjoyed, and you are meant to accept the enjoyment. Stop playing small and let yourself live the life that you yearn for. And if you are anything like me, your journey, like mine, hasn't been an easy or obvious one because I had no one modeling it for me. Be the change agent in your family, among your friends, or with anyone you influence.

POWER PRACTICES FOR SELF-WORTH

* Mind your mind and catch your thoughts on a daily basis.
* Look in the mirror, smile at yourself, and speak words of affirmation and kindness to yourself as a reminder of your worth.
* Every single time you walk out of your home, begin with a smile on your face and an affirmation on your heart, saying something to yourself like, "I am ready to be full on this glorious day."
* Always speak to yourself with great kindness.

DANCE WITH ME IN YOUR IMAGINATION

Let's imagine together you're walking around feeling the full measure of the life ordained upon you by the beloved Spirit that created all that is. Imagine living with a sense of yourself that allows you to fly high while at the same time be grounded in your greatest truth. The truth is that you are indeed a child of the beloved, one worthy beyond all explanation. Worthy of your good, your abundance, and your love.

JOURNAL PROMPTS

Write freely in your journal without editing or judging what you write. The freer you are with yourself, the more the wisdom will rise through you. Please don't think of these prompts as an assignment; think of them as a gentle exercise to expand your mind and open your heart. Ask yourself the following:

* How can I engage my world with a sense of self-worth greater than ever before?
* How will my self-talk change as I begin to know myself as worthy?
* What would my life look like if I fully embraced my inherent worthiness?
* What old beliefs about my worth no longer serve me, and what new beliefs am I ready to embrace?
* How has my sense of self-worth been shaped by past experiences and how can I reclaim my own definition of worth?
* If I spoke to myself with the same love and kindness I offer a dear friend, what would I say?
* What actions can I take daily to affirm and strengthen my self-worth?

A SPIRITUAL MINDSHIFT TO UPLEVEL YOUR SELF-WORTH

Sweet, delicious Spirit, I turn to you not as an outside authority but as a deep, indwelling friend who chooses to see me, play with me, and create through me. To this delicious Spirit, I call forth all aspects and qualities that I deserve to express and trust they will show up in, through, and as me.

I choose to boldly state that I am worthy. I am worthy of good, of love, of abundance, of health, of joy, of adventure, of profound satisfaction, and so much more. Never again shall I hang my self-worth upon the activities of my life, my education, or the approval of others. I fully declare that I am worthy without restriction and without exception.

I move beyond the limitations of my human self, I am the glorious essence that creates and sustains me, and so I am a worthy child of the Beloved One. Declaring my self-worth heals so many inner messages that I have been subscribing to for many years. I free myself from those messages and the conditioning they caused. I am more than that. God bless my parents who birthed me and did the best they could for me, but now it is my job, independent of my lineage, to declare the fullest expression of my worthiness that is possible.

To the power that creates, I say simply and directly that I am a worthy being, deserving and creating beyond anything I could possibly imagine.

And so it is.

An Extra Mindshift Affirmation for Self-Worth

There is a divine lover within me. That lover is my guide, my friend, and my authority. It dwells within the deepest part of my being, and yet it is not contained there; it is not contained at all. This is the very same essence that has created the stunning universe, its inhabitants, and all that moves and motivates us.

On this perfect day, I claim and declare that I choose to be true—true to the only self, the self that is who I truly am. I choose to be true to the part of me that seeks to be known not by other humans, but by my highest expression. I no longer look to my left or to my right. I no longer compare myself, nor do I seek any outside authority as a goal for being who I choose to be.

To my own self, I shall be true, devoted, and attentive in every loving way I can be. This love emanates from me with each word I speak, with each step I take, with every beat of my heart. With the bounty of gratitude for this invitation to express that inner self, I am truly grateful. I surrender this word right here, right now.

And so it is.

A LOVE LETTER TO MYSELF

Dearest Self,

Today, I honor you for the sacred and powerful journey you've taken on the path of self-worth.

There was a time when you questioned your value—when you tried to earn love, prove your importance, or become someone "better" just to feel enough. But slowly, steadily, you began to remember the truth: Your worth was never up for debate.

You are worthy, not because of what you do, achieve, or give, but because you are. Your existence is the evidence. You've stopped chasing approval and started claiming your space. You've learned to honor your needs, speak your truth, and set boundaries—not as a defense, but as an act of self-respect.

Your worth is no longer something you seek outside of you. It lives in your breath, your presence, your being. And now, you rise from that place with quiet power and radiant grace. I celebrate you for reclaiming this truth. May you continue to walk with the knowing that you are—and have always been—unquestionably worthy.

With reverence and deep love,
Me

REMEMBER TO BREATHE

Sit someplace quiet where you can be alone. Close your eyes and, with every breath you take over the next few minutes, feel the breath come and go from your body. Feel the process fully and completely while knowing you are worthy of all good all the time.

Let's Conclude with These Affirmations

- I now give myself permission to receive the bounty of my divine birthright.
- I now live a bold, brilliant, and stunning life expressing my worth in all moments.
- I am worthy of abundance, love, rest, joy, and all that nourishes my soul.
- **I demand to be me—without excuses.**

PEARLS OF WISDOM

If I've done my job well, by now your sense of self-worth has grown. You have begun to remember who you are and that you are worthy. Activating your self-worth is not something that can be quickened by some trick of the mind. It takes cultivation and a regular returning to know this about yourself. I have been working with individuals for more than thirty years, and I assure you: You are not alone. I wish we did not share this self-doubt but we do, and yet it is not something we have to live with. We simply need to remember with each passing day and with each thought: *I am worthy. I am worthy of my divine birthright and all that comes with it.* And one of the very beautiful rewards of this authentic reality is that when you begin to activate this reality within yourself, you give permission for everyone else around you to also know it for themselves.

11

UNLEASHING THE FULL EXPRESSION OF YOUR SOUL

The Path of Self-Expression

Hold fast to dreams
For if dreams die
Life is a broken-winged bird
That cannot fly.
—**LANGSTON HUGHES**

DESCRIPTION OF SELF-EXPRESSION

Self-expression is the result of expressing the inspiration that is God-ordained without criticism or self-doubt. It results in the joy of being oneself in all of one's iterations.

HERE IS A QUICK START OPTION

Begin to free your imagination. Find outlets to express your creative side. (We all *have a creative side.) To express it, you must release all temptations to judge. Make it playful. Dance, sing, draw, cook, sculpt—anything that makes you wake up.*

I'm not an artist. I have no academic degree and very limited training in any one discipline, although I have spent the majority of my life working to understand myself and humanity at large. My self-expression is pure because it is less influenced by others. My self-expression is just that, an expression of the self that I choose to be. My lack of education occasionally gets in the way of my self-confidence but not nearly as much as it once did. While I am well-read in the realms of spirituality, metaphysics, and human development, these are books that academics might not appreciate or label as tools of an education. My limited exposure to other people's thoughts and opinions, such as those of recognized philosophers, caused me to uncover my own beliefs and inner wisdom.

Here is the beauty of looking within for my resources: Often, when I do discover something amazing that is part of the fabric of humanity, I find that others have said the very same thing, which affirms my confidence in my own discovery. I can celebrate the authentic source, wisdom, and genius of the universe and its generous nature as it makes itself available. You must learn to sit still long enough to capture it. Genius is all around you and ready for the picking. The beauty of this process is that, instead of always quoting others, you can find your own words and ideas, source from universal intelligence, and feel confident in your own inner wisdom.

To be fully expressed means that when you leave this planet you will do so all used up. You will go out on your terms, being ornery and filled with joy. Why slip out of this life in a quiet way? Go out with the cows' bells clanging in the hills and valleys. Be the crazy lady or the eccentric man that your neighbors talk about. Leave your mark on life by being you without excuses. Be the example of pure joy leaving nothing on the table, nothing undiscovered about yourself.

OPENING TO NEW CULTURES

There are so many musicians, poets, and twentysomething individuals in our culture today who are boldly fighting to live authentic lives—getting right in society's face about it. For those still attached to an older way of being, witnessing this cultural phenomenon might be unsettling. It may stir questions like: What's wrong with them? Why are they so bold, so loud, so pierced and tattooed? Why are their pants around their hips and their hair every color of the rainbow?

But for this creative, vibrant group, their authentic expression is nothing less than normal. They demand to be accepted as they are—and the beautiful thing is, they are just as committed to *you* being *you* as they are to themselves being fully seen. When these multicolored-haired, tattoo-bearing, pierced individuals began showing up in my world, I had to take a breath and learn how to be with it. I could feel my conditioned self rising with opinions and objections, and if it weren't for my deep commitment to unconditional love and acceptance, I might have gotten stuck there.

Having clear values that you're truly committed to will expand your thinking and open your heart to newness. As I stepped into curiosity and wonder, my world expanded—and suddenly it included this beautiful, dynamic generation of people. Beautiful, smart, loving individuals who showed up in my orbit to help me love and accept *myself* more fully.

In many ways, this bold and expressive generation gave me permission to express myself more freely—without apology. People who know me now know that I might show up in flowing purple clothing or mismatched patterns, with long blonde hair one day or short red hair the next. I show up as I am—because I finally allowed myself to be. I live more authentically now, with greater conviction and far less need to explain myself.

And you know what? I no longer feel discomfort walking in my own shoes—which are never heels anymore. Heels were the first thing to go when I started truly accepting myself.

While I am not an artist with any training, I am creative. The lack of training kept me feeling frustrated because I wanted to have the fun and enjoyment that I witnessed my artist friends having. They always looked as if they were enjoying life in ways that I could only witness. I watched my friends who painted, sculpted, wrote poetry and music, and performed as actors. What did they have that I didn't have? Was my life boring? Well, I was raising my sons, starting a ministry, and serving a middle-sized spiritual community, so I will give myself a bit of a break. I wasn't bored, but the missing was there.

The place where I did get to express myself creatively was on Sundays, during our celebrations. The pulpit along with the music and space was my palette. As I served to deliver a message, I did it in collaboration with others—yes, those artistic and creative individuals. I learned how to weave together their music, art, and spoken word to create impact in a way that would deliver the message, to make it memorable. The doors were wide open for me, and the artists were thrilled, as together we created magic. This creative magic opened minds and hearts and left many, including myself, in tears of joy as they were given license to express their most authentic selves. That stage, as we refer to it, became my place to be creative and express my heart.

Sadly, when Covid hit in 2019, our doors closed and my hands were tied. I am still mourning that loss, although my new creative expression is staring you in the face, for as one creative adventure ended, a new and wonderful door opened—being an author. Now I express myself through this spoken word. Trust me when I tell you that while I enjoy writing with the purpose of teaching concepts, never did I see in my future the identity of an author. I am glad to accept and embrace it, though.

In a way, with each book I write, it feels like leaving a conscious legacy of love. My most meaningful spiritual teacher died with her book still inside her, and I committed when she passed that I would not do that. But I also never expected for that which flows from me to be so fluid and plentiful.

My authentic creative expression could not be made possible without a significant commitment to self-acceptance and self-love. This is how all these parts play upon one another and create a synergistic whole—stunning, actually.

A number of years ago I decided to try and free up my creative side by doing something new, so I went and bought some oil pastels called Cray-Pas and quality paper and I began to doodle—yup—doodle. I figured, how could doodling ever be wrong? There in my chair alone at night, paper in lap and pastels at hand, I put Cray-Pas to paper, with the intention of freeing my imagination and not judging myself—the main thing: Do not judge—do not compare myself to anyone—just stay in my own lane and create—not for anyone but me and my own satisfaction.

What unfolded began to alter how I saw myself, because I found that sweet spot of nonjudgmental creativity. The mind can seriously get in the way of being creative when we let it. Over time I started producing some pieces that I was willing to hang up in my very public office, but I remained clear that they were for me and no one else. This of course didn't prevent comments and feedback. People said everything from "Aren't they beautiful!" to, "Oh, did the kids draw them?" It was fun to see demonstrated the concept that beauty is in the eye of the beholder.

The gift I received from taking the risk to explore something new and then the risk to display my work taught me that I didn't need agreement or approval from anyone. A fun little story: There was this one thing that happened. One of my friends who owned a flower shop decided to take some of my work and sell it in their store. *What a silly idea*, I thought, and I was so surprised when she sold every piece that she displayed. WHAT?! Oh my—my doodles had value. Who knew?

A wise teacher who has inspired me, Ernest Holmes, wrote in his most meaningful textbook a three-word sentence that I have taken to heart: "Create or perish." The first time I read those three words, they struck me deep in my soul and pushed me to free my creative side even more. It made sense to me that we each have an urge to create from deep within us. How could we not? If we each are a child of the Beloved Creative Source of Life, and if we agree that the Beloved's inspiration and intelligence creates through you, then you must be the evidence of this creative legacy. It is logical that continuing to express the divine creative urge keeps you fully involved in the beauty of life.

You might already be aware of this, but once people become adults, they will often lie about themselves and their creativity. They'll say they are not an artist, but that is another inauthentic, conditioned response. As a child, creativity flowed out of you like a waterfall, natural, easy, and effortless; but as you grew, so did your opinions, judgments, and tendencies to compare yourself. And there is nothing that will suppress your creative side more than these habits, especially comparison. When you compare yourself to another, you will always lose.

> ***I am a feminist, and what that means to me is much the same as the fact that I am Black. It means that I must undertake to love myself and to respect myself as though my very life depends upon self-love and self-respect.***

THE TOXIC INFLUENCE OF SOCIAL MEDIA

The social media phenomenon has only increased our tendency to wear masks and to be inauthentic. Social media platforms are an endless opportunity for self-criticism, competition, and self-denial like nothing we have ever seen. At any given time, there exists a relentless number of "influencers" ready and waiting to tell you what you need, how you need to look, what you need to buy, how you need to be—so you can be just as wonderful as they are. If you have never seen them, good for you; that means that your algorithm is keeping you safe. But imagine giving your preteen a phone without restrictions. What a hazard this would become because that young, easily influenced mind is just ready to want and be what they are not.

We live our choices every moment of every day, whether we are aware of it or not. Every day your focus and attention are their own algorithm of sorts. This algorithm becomes conditioned by your interests and attention. You have within your reach the power to call forth an experience that expresses the life you choose; but for you and anyone you influence, this does require you to be more conscious. The more aware you are of all the surrounding influences, the more you live at choice. And if you are anything like me and want to leave this world a better place, start with yourself and grow brightly so who you are matters more and more and everyone around you benefits from your growth.

Let's protect our children. Preteens live at the mercy of conditions outside of themselves, and the teen suicide rate in the United States is the third-leading cause of death. Perhaps even more surprising, in 2022 the male suicide rate was four times higher than that of females. I use the word *surprising* because we are often so rightly worried about our daughters being influenced by social media and marketing, but less often do we consider our sons as being at risk of these same influences.

Until one can thoroughly discriminate about what they are viewing, they should not be given access to these sources of influence. Some say do not give children a phone with internet access until the age of fourteen, and I agree with that idea. Please take this warning seriously because there are individuals out there with evil intent and they are ready to groom your son or daughter toward their own needs. To protect our children from harm, we must surface their disapproval of our rules. Let them be mad; they will understand when they are older.

As I spoke about earlier in the book about our addiction to being liked, social media is a definite expression in the most literal way of measuring our okayness through the amount of likes we can garner. And for those young and very impressionable minds, the likes are way more important than their authentic expression. They don't care how they get them; they aren't concerned with being real or honest. After all, there are AI apps that can make you look taller, thinner, clearer skinned, and with really great hair. Who needs to worry when you can simply fake the reality of you?

When these young people mature and begin to have children and grandchildren of their own, a new reality is going to hit them hard. There will come a time when they realize the world they created is not a world they want to raise their own children in. Once a child's attention is captured by the avenue of social media, it is very difficult to uncouple them from it because they have been receiving dopamine hits through their incessant scrolling. The same for those who create these memes and reels, it is all about the hits of dopamine that comes every time someone hits like.

And clearly this applies for us as adults. Social media offers a dangerous dopamine drip camouflaged as news and amusement. Trusting anything you see or read on social media is downright insane. If it were only populated with honest information, and AI was not a thing, well maybe we could trust it more for the source of amusement that it used to be. As I author this book, I am told to stay aware of my social media platforms as a source for sales of the book. So, while I might want to avoid it, my publisher encourages me to grow my audience.

And true confessions here, as an author and a teacher, social media is part of my reality and I will openly admit to you that when I first began to post on social media, I would post something and then incessantly watch for who liked me. Oh my, my self-worth was being measured by likes. How pathetic is that! Gratefully I have come away from needing that feedback.

It makes me wonder how the great authors and orators of the past century became the phenomenon that they did without these platforms.

Social media is a completely contrived form of communication, which we need to not give our power to. You as the authentic, beautiful, and powerful being that you are does not need anything outside of you to feel the fullness of your being. And just like Don Miguel Ruiz taught us in *The Four Agreements*, his chapter on not taking things personally—anything or anyone that can make you feel better about yourself can also make you feel worse.

Take your power back by not subscribing to the demands of social media to be what you are not.

POWER PRACTICES FOR SELF-EXPRESSION

- Stop any kind of criticism when you are ready to be creative or solve a problem.
- Allow your mind to be open by asking questions like: What wants to be created here?
- Take time to have fun creating. Choose any kind of arts and crafts. Commit to doing something fun and creative at least once a week.
- Go on a date with a friend or alone to a place that inspires

you: a museum, musical performance, or local theater—as long as you feel inspired by it.

- Make a create date. Remember the knitting circles during times of war that grew into clubs of friends? Find others with a similar interest and spend time creating together.
- Learn some new craft. There are free resources all over the internet. It is how I taught myself to practice Zentangle and to make paper. Free and fun.

DANCE WITH ME IN YOUR IMAGINATION

Well, isn't this the perfect time to use our imagination in the most creative way possible?

Picture the walls of your home adorned with your own art or crafts or envision yourself playing an instrument, or possibly writing a new song for your instrument. Imagine the joy on your face each time you sit down to create something. Imagine it so vividly that you can feel the sense of satisfaction and delight. Now, expand that vision. Think of yourself as part of a vibrant community, a group of people all sharing in the power of creative expression. See the smiles, feel the joy, and recognize that you are a co-creator of beauty.

How might the world shift if more of us focused on the possibilities of self-expression rather than the weight of stress and problems? Now, take it further—imagine encouraging your children, nieces, or nephews to explore their own creativity. Beauty and creativity have a purpose, even if that purpose is simply to exist. And what a beautiful world that would be.

Imagine drawing not inside the lines but on a blank canvas. Be your bold self—unapologetically.

JOURNAL PROMPTS

Write freely in your journal without editing or judging what you write. The freer you are with yourself, the more the wisdom will rise through you. Ask yourself:

- What would change in my life if I allowed myself to be more creative?
- How would I allow myself to be more creative as I began to stop criticizing myself?
- Might there be other aspects of myself that I would discover if I finally freed my self-expression?
- What has caused me to pause?
- Why have I not picked up my guitar (or any instrument)?
- Why have I not begun to knit, crotchet, draw, cook, or sew again?
- As I allow myself to be more fully expressed, what might change in my life?

A SPIRITUAL MINDSHIFT AFFIRMATION TO UPLEVEL YOUR SELF-EXPRESSION

The holy, sacred, indwelling Spirit of creativity that not only created me but lives within me even now, creates out of Itself through me and as me—and to that I surrender.

I may call this power by many names, but no matter the name, I remain a joyful and open recipient of Its influence. In my openness, I accept it as the inspiration in all areas of my life. I accept it as the authority of creativity in who I am. And in this acceptance, as I allow It, It chooses to express itself through me.

I enthusiastically create and express myself through all my actions, practices, writing, and speaking. My creative self-expression is beautiful and stunning, and I am inspired by how this creative essence moves through me.

Joy is my reward for allowing this to happen. Joy—spontaneous, profound moments of joy—is the deep reward that shows itself to me daily simply because I get my bloated nothingness out of the way, allowing my expression freedom.

With profound gratitude for the universal laws that respond to my spoken word, I am grateful and so I release this word to be fully demonstrated.

And so it is.

A LOVE LETTER TO MYSELF

Dearest Self,

Today, I celebrate the freedom you've found on the path of self-expression. What a beautiful unfolding it's been—this journey of allowing your true voice to rise, your creativity to flow, your essence to be seen and heard.

There was a time when you held back, unsure if your words mattered, afraid your truth would be too much or not enough. But now, you are learning to speak from the heart, show up fully, and create without apology.

You are now willing to be in the dance of life—with or without music, but highly tuned to the rhythm of the universe.

You've discovered that your voice is not something to be perfected; it is something to be honored. Whether through words, art, movement, or quiet presence, you've begun to let the real you come forward.

You no longer wait for permission. You no longer dim to fit. Instead, you express what's within you—because it's yours to share, and the world is better for it.

I celebrate you for daring to be seen and heard. May you continue to express yourself with authenticity, courage, and joy. Your truth is a gift.

With love and encouragement,
Me

REMEMBER TO BREATHE

Let's have some fun. With some music playing in the background, stand up, then bend over, and with your arms make a motion as if scooping up a whole boatload of anything. Lift your arms up over your head as if in celebration. Take a big breath while doing this, and on the exhalation exclaim, "I am here, I am ready, I am stunning!" Say it as you release the breath and do it again and again.

There is real value in combining the breath and your spoken word. It helps to bring your truth into your body temple.

Let's Conclude with These Affirmations

- I give myself permission to express my truth with clarity, creativity, and courage.
- I honor my voice, my art, my laughter, my rage, whatever is real.
- I refuse to shrink to fit anyone else's comfort.
- **I demand to be me—without excuses.**

PEARLS OF WISDOM

If you're anything like me, you might think you're not an artist—but being an artist and being creative are two different things. Making room for your very beautiful and individual self-expression is one of the most creative things you can do for yourself.

To find a way to free your creativity—and to be willing to express it without judging it—will free up energy inside of you that will support your joy, health, love, and interactions with the people around you.

It doesn't matter what it is—just find something you enjoy doing creatively, and do it. I don't care if you buy crayons and a coloring book—just do it. If you're all about plants and horticulture—do it. If you want to learn how to play the piano, or you already play—do it. If you're a poet or a wannabe poet—just write, and do it.

Self-expression is one of the most beautiful gifts we can give ourselves, and one of the quickest paths to our authenticity that we have.

12

LOVE YOURSELF LIKE YOUR LIFE DEPENDS ON IT

The Path of Self-Love

How you love yourself is how you teach others to love you.

—RUPI KAUR

Description of Self-Love

Self-love is the beautiful aggregate of believing in oneself completely as a child of the Beloved One, born in purity, no matter the circumstances, and feeling this love so deeply and profoundly that it causes one to walk this planet with beauty, ease, and grace.

Here Is a Quick Start Option

Write this down and hang it in numerous places, so you can see it throughout your day and say it out loud with great emotion: ***I am a child of the beautiful, loving, creative, intelligence of the universe.*** *(This is not ego—ego stands for edging God out. This is truth.) This is the goal and the reward for all your inner cultivating, looking, inquiring, and forgiving. It is the zest to be your spiritual authentic self.*

As I have established already, there is no private good. *No private good* simply means that as you grow and heal, you become a greater influence for the whole planet, beginning with your family. You, your changes, and your healing ripple out to impact everyone around you. We are a beautiful reflection of one another, and the more we love ourselves in a whole way, the more room we make to love those around us; and as we model this way of being, we give permission for others to follow suit.

The chapter-opening quote by Rupi Kaur is more than wise and beautiful; it is a spiritual principle that is created and experienced through us. To the degree that you are willing to take responsibility for your life and to increase your self-love, you will know the world. If love is not part of the formula, you might just see the world as dark, dismal, and a sad place to be, but increase your self-love quotient and you will see the world through the eyes of love, acceptance, and wonder, beautiful wonder.

A dedication and adherence to increased self-love in its purest form causes us to see through a filter so pure that our world instantly looks more beautiful, just like seeing through rose-colored glasses. As you subscribe to self-love, your world begins to reflect that love back to you almost immediately. Others, who have not yet committed to raising their self-love quotient, will wonder why you think the world is beautiful. They might wonder why you accept instead of reject people of different backgrounds; they might be confused by the level of your interest, curiosity, and acceptance of others. That is because they cannot see what you can see because they are caught in the world of effects.

Those who dance along the path of certainty of love, beauty, and joy could be seen as masters and gurus, but in truth, they are simply living the life we were born to live and living it authentically. From this point of view, joy can be a constant and real reward.

As we deepen our self-love and begin to view the world through that lens, we also become a *cause* of beauty in the world. My understanding of quantum science suggests to me that the world we perceive is a reflection of our observations and intentions. In other words, **what we focus on, we**

help bring into form. This is not unlike raising children. When a child is nurtured with love, kindness, and acceptance, they tend to internalize that voice and reflect it back into the world. On the other hand, when a child is raised in an environment of harshness, criticism, and judgment, it often gives rise to self-doubt and a distorted sense of self-worth. The voices around us shape the voices within us, and self-love begins by changing the tone of that inner dialogue, one thought and one inner dialogue at a time, which is why we began this book with self-talk.

> ***If we give our children sound self-love, they will be able to deal with whatever life puts before them.***
>
> **—BELL HOOKS**

Without self-love you are doomed to fall into the trap of believing what the world believes about you, what you feel it says about you, and what it might even say directly to your face.

Self-love is not the self-centered act that it is so often labeled to be. Self-love is a survival tool, and your relationship with yourself is the only one that can save your life. You are never truly alone, but that does not prevent you from feeling lonely. In your loneliest of moments, self-love is the only love that can fill that vast emptiness that we all feel when we forget who we are. When life throws challenges at you, it is your self-love that will lift you, embrace you, and comfort you. Developing it might not be easy, but it will save your life, your heart, and your relationship with the rest of the world around you.

As you begin your quest to understand and expand your self-love, it's important to know that the path to getting there is not a straight one. The path might just bob and weave, and in my experience and of those I've taught over the years, it is populated with many distractions along the way. Self-love is, in a way, the magic cure for many emotional and physical ailments. Along that path, you will come face-to-face with your demons, self-judgments, and self-doubts. You might be shocked and overwhelmed by the amount of limited-thinking habits you have in addition to your self-beliefs and stories you tell yourself that are blocking your path. *PRESS ON.* Don't believe what you see, don't give your power away, and don't believe what the world might tell you.

To love the self of you is to love God (or Spirit, Life, Energy, or Intelligence) *as* you. That love, that pure essence, is the only true healing salve that exists, because that love seeps deep within your being and will carry you when times are tough; and times will be tough. If you are engaging the world and have a grand idea for yourself, the path for your life will be filled with opportunities to get to know yourself more (in other words, to overcome challenges). When relationships get tough, your self-love will be there to remind you of who you are.

If you are struggling, you are probably being called to do some forgiveness work. The struggle is an indication that you believe *something, or someone, is against you.* Your forgiveness practice will help you to take your power back and allow your self-love to be your authority once again. Then you will be available to love others more completely.

How do you love what appears to be unlovable? Think of the forest that gives season after season; think of the mother who loves her children unconditionally even when they forget to call; think of victims of serious crime who choose to forgive their offender so they themselves can be free. No one *outside* of you is against you. If it appears that way, turn within, look for that place of beauty, power, and source that was born with you. It is right there at the center of your being—don't let anyone tell you otherwise. Self-love is another way of loving the creator as you. God, Spirit, Life, Energy, or Intelligence demands nothing in return for Its unending love and grace. I believe that self-love is the only quest worthy of your time and attention. You are worthy of the bounty of self-love.

Go and *be love,* my beloved. Go and be love.

How Do You Increase Your Self-Love Quotient?

I am so glad you asked, and my answer might seem a bit backward, but in truth the path that you choose to journey along was never going to be a straight line.

Increasing your self-love is as much about stopping some old habits as starting new ones. And you will notice that many of these practices have already been included in other areas of this book. Again, this is because of their importance and because humans are quite stubborn when it comes to making changes. While I hope this book offers you a gentle path, walk it boldly, demand change of yourself, and expect transformation. Walk this path, dance this dance courageously. Please continue to remember throughout that you are worthy of this work you have invested in.

Below is a list of new thinking and being habits along which to travel to raise your self-love quotient. These are meant to replace your life-limiting habits that we share but can go unnoticed because we have normalized them by not challenging them.

As always, while you read this list, be gentle with yourself. Even if you recognize yourself in each habit, be gentle, kind, and patient with yourself. I offer you this guidance to support your freedom—and it should never be used to beat yourself up.

To make this more palatable as you read the list below, think about it within this context: How free can I be as I release this habit? Or, who do I want to be when I cease this way of being? Or, how brilliant and extraordinary could my life be if I no longer entertained these habits?

Here is a short, solid list of new habits to support this leg of your journey:

1. Cease All Negative Self-Talk: As you can see, my very first reminder takes us back to the beginning of this book and that is because we must walk the path to our authentic self as a whole and not in parts. It's time to address how harsh your inner dialogue is and how it erodes your self-love. It is time to discipline yourself by replacing it with affirmations or compassionate self-talk. (This takes us back to self-inquiry and self-contemplation.)

    * Who do I get to be when my self-talk is self-loving?

2. Perfectionism: Explore the idea of letting go of the need to be perfect and embrace the beauty of imperfection as part of being human. If you only love the parts of you that humanity would

measure as acceptable, you might find yourself quite limited; your job is to love every cell of your being, even if it does not fall into the category of "perfect" by outside standards—or even your own standards that have likely been influenced by others. Truthfully, the goal is to not care about anyone's opinions but your own.

- Who do I get to be when I completely accept myself just as I am?

3. People-Pleasing: Begin to set boundaries and learn to prioritize yourself over seeking external validation. As we learned earlier, setting boundaries is an expression of self-care, and it is critical to feeling safe in the world to express yourself unconditionally.

   - Who do I get to be when I stop trying to please others and just live within my own standards?

4. Comparisons: When you compare, you lose—it is as simple as that. Comparing is a sneaky little habit that can happen very quickly without notice. This is one of those times when it is especially important to pay close attention to your body's reaction, because your mind might attempt to justify what you are noticing. It is through your body that you will recognize that you feel insignificant as you compare yourself to another.

   Comparison can also cause us to strive more or to be more competent in our skills, but it is a slippery slope. Be careful. If you want to use it mindfully, go ahead, but please dear precious reader, never allow it to bring you down.

   - Who do I get to be as I cease the habit of comparing myself to others?

5. Part A. Over-Accepting Responsibility: As a teacher and a coach of forgiveness, shadow work, and self-empowerment, I encourage

those I support to take responsibility for their lives. You cannot influence any change in your life that you have not first taken responsibility for.

But there is a significant difference between taking responsibility or ownership for your life and taking responsibility for more than what you have created. This is what happens when one is abused. The abused often takes the responsibility for being available to the abuser even if they were only a child.

Part B. We are here to learn how to respond to all aspects of our life but not to take the blame for the breaking down of things that are outside our control. Over-accepting responsibility is almost self-abuse because when you over-accept, you suffer.

* Who do I get to be when I take responsibility for my life?

6. Stop Dwelling on Past Mistakes: Humans have incessant, habitual ways of thinking. We regurgitate conversations, specifically upsetting conversations ad nauseam without paying attention to the impact it has on our mental, emotional, and physical health. This habit gets propagated through gossip and incessant storytelling about your woes. To love yourself is to let yourself off the hook. Stop fertilizing the seeds of self-doubt, criticism, fear, and mistakes by the retelling of your errors. You deserve to forgive yourself once and for all and release yourself from the weight of all those stories.

    * Who do I get to be as I learn to let go of past mistakes and choose to live in this present moment?

I learned a very long time ago that cultivating my self-love was the most worthy use of my time and attention, because the tiny tastes I had of that self-love were transformative. You see, when you love yourself, it changes how you see the world. Your entire worldview is impacted—and since our worldview is what we create through, it's extraordinary how loving myself has changed the way I show up and how much love I've received as a result of that shift.

And since the name of this book is *Dance Like Nobody's Watching*, consider this: When you want to dance—even if you don't care what someone else thinks about your dancing—learning a few basic steps gives you more freedom and choice. It's like the musician who studies classical styles for years, only to become a rock and roller. Once you've gained the skills, that's when you can throw out the rule book and have a great time.

What I discovered for myself and would love for you to discover for yourself is how freaking beautiful the world is when you see through a new set of loving eyes.

THE REWARDS FOR GOING HOME TO YOUR AUTHENTIC SELF

My teaching and my books are all created to invite individuals to regain their personal power, self-respect, and self-love, but the path to getting there is not necessarily easy while it is massively rewarding.

The closer you move toward your authentic self, the easier you can breathe and just be. I mean this literally. There are times in your day when you suddenly take an extra big breath. This breath means you were not breathing fully, and it is often the result of silent stress, the kind that you don't notice until you do. You get to breathe deeper and more fully because you do not need to feel guarded. And if you think I am overselling this idea, talk to someone with COPD or another issue with their lungs. Your breath is one of the greatest gifts, and it is a gift because it is given to you automatically, since you don't have to stop and think to yourself, *Oh yeah, I should breathe now.*

Another wonderful gift that is supported by you breathing fully is a sense of relaxation. When you no longer need to protect yourself or project a false face through darned masks, you can actually let go of the load of stress it takes to present your fake self.

You regain energy when you strip the fake parts of you and show up authentically. All these things begin to add up, you breathe easier, walk around more relaxed in your body temple, and you relax more fully because you have freed yourself from pretense.

When you return home to your authentic self, you also regain your personal power. This is the reward for building your self-confidence as you learn to trust yourself and believe in yourself.

One of the bigger surprises of going home to your authentic self is knowing who you are so completely that you won't need to take things personally. And if someone does try to tear you down, you will have the confidence to ignore them completely.

POWER PRACTICES FOR SELF-LOVE

- Practice being gentle with yourself.
- Treat yourself as you would a newborn baby.
- Write a letter to your future self and project loving support and kindness for yourself.

DANCE WITH ME IN YOUR IMAGINATION

Imagine a world where people truly, honestly, and completely love and accept themselves—not in an egotistical way, but in a way that reflects their deep knowing that they are divine offspring, worthy of all good.

Now imagine if every interaction you have is with people who embody this truth—people who move through life with self-assurance, kindness, and grace. How brilliant would the world be if every encounter felt like a secret, beautiful meeting filled with curiosity, love, and smiles?

Picture a highway where drivers make space for one another

with ease and consideration. Envision a world where we no longer pressure our sons and daughters to be something they're not but instead honor and celebrate who they already are.

And what if social media became a space of genuine kindness and encouragement, free from comparison or the need to prove or be anything other than our most authentic selves?

This is the world we could create with a shift in consciousness. Can you imagine it?

JOURNAL PROMPTS

Ask yourself:

- What would life look like and feel like if I truly loved myself unconditionally?
- How will I parent, lead, or instruct those under my influence as I learn to love my whole life expression?
- What might become possible for me and my family if I shifted how I saw myself in the mirror?
- What choices would I make differently if love was my guide and not my self-deprecated habits?

A SPIRITUAL MINDSHIFT AFFIRMATION FOR SELF-LOVE

Looking beyond the human ego that I recognize as an influencer in my life, I choose to love my ego and myself absolutely and completely. I move beyond the framework of my human ego. I choose to love myself because I know that my choice is required to move into alignment with the loving presence that is. This choice is essential because so many things are constantly seeking my attention. I choose to love the all of me, the more of me, the not-yet-expressed of me. I choose to love the aspects of me that are easy to enjoy, and I choose to love the aspects of me in which I have faulted, denied, and judged. This transformation is made by refocusing my attention on self-love.

Because I know there is no private good, I understand that my self-love opens the door to being a presence of love for others. This is a holy and sacred calling. My heart and mind resonate to express this beautiful and powerful truth of who I am.

This is all made possible because I have learned to surrender my human will to my spiritual essence. I surrender everything—all concern, resistance, and fear of my light. Never again shall I fear my greatness. I am ready to allow the universal love that exists in all humans and all forms of existence to be my guiding source.

And so it is.

A LOVE LETTER TO MYSELF

Dearest Self,

Today, I bow to the journey you've taken on the path of self-love. This is the path that changes everything—the path that brings you home.

There was a time when you stood on the outside of your own heart, waiting to be invited in. You gave love freely to others yet struggled to offer it to yourself. But something in you knew that your healing, joy, and wholeness could only grow from love that starts within.

And so, you began. Gently at first, then more boldly, you turned toward yourself with tenderness. You stopped abandoning yourself in hard moments. You learned to hold space for your pain, celebrate your light, and nourish your soul with presence and care.

Self-love became less of a concept and more of a practice—a daily act of devotion—in the way you speak to yourself, the choices you make, and how you show up for your needs and honor your boundaries.

You've learned that loving yourself isn't selfish—it's sacred. It's the root from which all other love grows.

I celebrate you for choosing this path. May you continue to walk it with grace, knowing that you are—always and forever—worthy of your own love. I love you dearly.

With all my heart,
Me

REMEMBER TO BREATHE

We have come to end of our time together, but you have just begun your journey. Remember with each breath you breathe to affirm, "I love myself as I am." Use your breath to grow your self-love.

Let's Conclude with These Affirmations

- I give myself permission to love myself fully, deeply, and without conditions.
- I become my own sanctuary, my own source of radical love.
- I am the place where love resides.
- **I demand to be me—without excuses.**

PEARLS OF WISDOM

I am not so bold to claim that I am your spiritual teacher at this time, but I will share with you that my original and most significant spiritual teacher, who I loved with all my heart, always spoke of raising one's self-love quotient. If you have read, practiced, journaled, used the mindshifts, read the letters to yourself, taken time to get quiet and contemplate, and make great inquiries into the self of your being, then I bet you have found a wealth of untapped reasons for your own self-love. The journey inward is rife with reasons to love yourself. And through this journey you didn't create new reasons; you just got rid of the distractions. You, once again, my dear reader, are a stunning and beautifully worthy individual of your own self-love. I hope I have encouraged you to feel that and to believe in that and to accept that at the level of your soul.

APPENDIX

Guidelines for a Silent Retreat

As you begin reading this appendix, I want to drive home a point: **Silence is truly your best friend** when it comes to creating meaningful and lasting change in your life.

Guided meditations are wonderful—some are deeply potent and can absolutely spark transformation. But when you become truly comfortable with silence itself, it nurtures you in a deeper way. Silence helps you become more at ease in your own skin and more aligned with your unique way of being.

While this book is meant to be an invitation to be your bold, beautiful, and fully expressed self, to dance like nobody's watching means you need to first dance in the safety of your inner landscape—as the person you were meant to be. First, we go inside so we can then express outside.

When you commit to a regular practice of silence, the world around you begins to shift. It feels less hostile, more spacious. You find yourself less reactive to the noise—the fearmongering in the news and the emotional static of social media. Silence is a gift we give ourselves, a sacred pause that allows us to remember who we are.

It is no accident that silence sits at the heart of so many spiritual traditions. Spiritual teachers and religious leaders alike encourage silence as a response to life's challenges and anxiety. It offers depth, wisdom, and quiet reassurance for the journey you're on.

And my friend, whether you feel ready or not, you do have what it takes. You already hold the wisdom, knowledge, and confidence needed to make powerful, authentic changes in your life.

Silence simply helps you uncover what's already within you.

The following represents what I believe and have taught for years, which I am adapting from a guide I wrote years ago: Become comfortable with silence and you will tap into your authentic, intelligent, and most inspired self.

There is a vast resource within you waiting to be discovered, but it is silence that opens the door to that inner vault of knowledge. The key to unlock it is *calm—deep profound calm.* Finding comfort in silence is that invitation. Therein between the words, right where you are, God is, peace prevails, and love reigns!

Everything that matters—peace, love, inspiration, intuition, confidence, and more—exists right where you are. I'm certain that this is not the first time that you have been told this, but it is possible that you have never been given a road map before.

This guide is a road map to the wealth of brilliance that already exists within you—the same brilliance that resides in every human being. This means that everyone around you has the potential to inspire you, reflecting your own gifts and genius back to you. Your brilliance lies beyond the chatter of your mind, waiting to be uncovered. Investing your time, focus, and attention in your healing, transformation, and spiritual practice is essential. Personal inquiry, contemplation, and moments of silence are not just beneficial—they are necessary parts of your journey.

Simply said, to hear your own brilliance, you must listen, and being in silence is the one amazing way to hear! Listen, inquire, contemplate, pray, and practice forgiveness and silence. This is a cocktail for your human, spiritual transformation!

You are holding in your hands a self-guided silent retreat.

Not everyone is ready to retreat at one of those well-known ten-day free silent retreats, so here is another option. Maybe you want to put your toe in the water first. This is an opportunity to do it in your own home. This self-guided silent retreat will give you a wonderful first taste of silence. Included is a list of tips and supportive ideas to help pave the way. The purpose is to set you up for a renewing experience by anticipating some of the distractions that are unique to you and how to prepare yourself to handle them in advance. If this really is your FIRST time in extended silence, you will really want to pay attention to the list of preparations. In addition, I will provide questions to ponder and stimulate your inner contemplation and some techniques to practice.

The intention here: Set yourself up for success!

THIS IS VERY IMPORTANT!

Prepare for your time of silence.

1. Begin by choosing the length of time. Try investing Friday night through Sunday or, if that's too long, just do one night. If you have an unconventional job or you are retired, you get to choose freely what works for you.

   Note: You may consider scheduling your retreat to either celebrate a significant birthday, an anniversary of the beginning of a new venture, or by saying goodbye to a loved one.
2. Add up the number of meals that you would normally eat during the chosen length of time and plan to have enough food in the house so you do not have to go out or order in. The goal is seclusion.

   A new experience like this might spark your insecurities, making you think that you are hungry. Don't overload on any kind of junk food. Keep it healthy. You wouldn't want to feed that inner child and get distracted from your purpose.
3. Tell your friends and family that you will not be available during this time and ask them not to contact you unless it is urgent.
4. Plan on temporarily changing your voicemail announcement and email auto-reply with a message stating you are unavailable. Yes, I am suggesting that you keep your computer shut off or at the very least OFFLINE. By communicating your intentions in advance, people will be more likely to give you the space to explore this side of you, and to do that, you need significant alone time.

5. Physically unplug your television. If you normally enjoy a bit of television, unplugging it will help you resist the temptation to watch.
6. Stop drinking caffeine at least one to two days in advance. Let your body become calm. Have some herbal and soothing teas available.
7. Have your journal, pens, pencils, and coloring pencils at the ready. Silence can spark your creativity; allow this to happen WITHOUT getting too busy or overly involved. The purpose of journaling or drawing is to capture your silent inspirations, not to fill the time with busyness.
8. If this is your first time and silence seems impossible, go ahead and prepare yourself with some music. If you use a streaming service, search either meditation music or reiki music, but most definitely music without words. In the Resources section I suggest some specific music that might work for you.
9. Clean your home before you begin. This is for two reasons: First, so you can relax into your home as your own sanctuary. Second, so you do not begin to clean if you find yourself "bored."
10. Should you decide to use this retreat for the purpose of a transformational time, you might want to create a ritual for yourself. In that case, have some candles and incense available. White sage is used to cleanse stale or old energy and burning it is called *smudging*. Smudging is a good ritual.

Set Your Intentions Before You Begin

Begin your time with self by setting your intention. Ask yourself this question before you begin and then set your intention accordingly: Who do I want to be at the close of this time of silence?

Be mindful with setting your intentions. Set an intention that will create the most powerful experience possible. A well-stated intention will act as the thread that pulls you through the weekend and draws to you everything you were looking for, even if your intention is to be in a state of surrender.

You might want to try something like this:

* I remain open to discovering untapped strengths, talents, and creativity deep within the silence of my soul.
* I am ready for the fullness of my being to be revealed.
* I surrender to stillness, allowing wisdom to rise from the depths of my soul.
* In silence, I create space for divine insight and clarity to unfold.
* I trust that the quiet reveals what words cannot.
* I embrace silence as a gateway to my deepest truth and highest potential.
* Through stillness, I attune to the rhythm of my inner knowing.
* I rest in the sacred hush, where all I need is already present.
* In the quiet, I listen—not only with my ears, but with my heart and soul.
* I honor silence as a sacred path to self-discovery and transformation.
* I allow stillness to dissolve distractions and guide me to what truly matters.
* Through silence, I reconnect with the infinite source of love, wisdom, and peace within me.

Here are some affirmations to support your inner journey:

* I surrender into this silence fully and allow the inspiration of this universe to comfort me.
* With each hour of silence, I am moved deeper into my inner landscape as I reap my divine wisdom and intuition.
* In my silence, my resolve is strengthened and freed for expression.

When I attend any retreat weekend, no matter what the purpose of the retreat, I launch my time by setting my own intentions. So, through my own intent, I cultivate an atmosphere that is rich with intentional rewards.

Your intention can be as simple as intending to be in a state of surrender in which you allow for whatever needs to come to arrive with ease and grace.

You might want to set the intention to reawaken your own inspiration or renew your creative outlet, whatever that is for you. Don't be surprised if you find yourself either feeling deeply grounded and relaxed or highly energized and inspired. Either could happen depending upon who you are.

Things to Ponder

- What is mine to do in this life?
- What are my gifts to be revealed and shared?
- What have I been holding as the reason(s) for playing small in this world?
- With whom must I practice forgiveness to be free?
- What can I forgive myself for to be free?
- Which of God's gifts have I yet to demonstrate in my life?
- What distractions must be freed so I can reveal from within me the abundant resources of inspiration?
- When I leave this world, what will I be known for?

  (Writing your own eulogy is an interesting exercise when you want to determine who you are in the world.)
- What makes my heart sing?
- Where can I love more?
- If I leave one impression in this world that is uniquely mine, what is it?

Dealing with Those Demons!

There is an interesting thing that begins to happen as we practice silence. At times, we might hear a cacophony of inner voices that is the accumulation of a lifetime of judgments of both self and others; this is the conditioning of humanity, our lineage, and our nuclear family, plus more.

Initially it can be so loud that you will not be able to imagine how you never heard it before. This is one of the effects of silence that will have many individuals not wanting to practice silence. *Just be prepared.* However, it is the greatest gift that you will receive from your invested time. As you close your mouth and listen, voices—yours and others—will become audible. Your inner thoughts will not feel "inner" anymore. The room will become filled with your own inner community. Once you begin to hear them, you can free yourself from the ones that do not serve you.

REMEMBER, INQUIRY AND CONTEMPLATION LEAD TO AWARENESS. AWARENESS CAN BE IN AND OF ITSELF CURATIVE, AND THIS LEADS TO YOUR OWN PERSONAL EVOLUTION.

The awareness of the problem is the beginning of its solution.
—JIDDU KRISHNAMURTI

This is the good news, albeit challenging: The gift of silence is the relief you feel from not having to be your personality. When you can finally let go and just be, an overall relaxation will come over you, and you will feel free enough to hear all those voices.

Take time to journal about what you hear. There's no rush, and you will deal with all of it, one thought at a time.

The demons are not really demons; they are the evidence of your soul freeing itself from your human condition. Just as the voices of judgment are contained within, so are the voices of wisdom, forgiveness, and self-love. Silence is the path that will lead you through the cacophony to the sound of ease and grace, self-love, and unconditional self-acceptance.

BE FEARLESS: This is the process!

Practicing forgiveness!

Of course, I am going to include forgiveness in these instructions for silence. It is important because so much of the business and chaos and lack of calm that we experience in our daily lives is the result of the stories that we hold on to and continue to suffer from. These emotions get very loud as your silence grows deep. Be not afraid: You have what is needed to heal from your stories and trauma. It all lives within.

We forgive others, not to free them of their own karmic debt, but to free ourselves from being their jailer. We forgive ourselves because we remember that we are a child of the One and this One never wants us to suffer. Forgiveness is our pathway to freedom. Forgiving others has nothing to do with them. It has only to do with our freedom. We forgive so we may live the life that is ours. The law of compensation will take care of everyone else.

Forgiveness is a big subject, one that we can only begin to touch upon in this book. I mention it anyway, because without a forgiveness practice in place you won't be prepared to deal with some of the unsettling voices that free themselves during your silence.

For so many people in this Western culture of ours, silence is simply not within our typical realm of experience. Neither is a healthy conversation regarding forgiveness or self-forgiveness. True forgiveness happens over a period of time; it will happen in layers and so it is not something that can be completed in any single weekend. When someone asks the question, "How do you know if you need to forgive?," we, who teach forgiveness, will often answer the question by offering a follow-up question: "Are you breathing?"

There will be indicators that things are shifting along the way, such as certain relationships changing and stress between you and another easing up. You will be able to experience this shift in many ways, including paying attention to your body temple. Indicators could be anything from feeling relaxed and free to exuberant and energized. As we release the weight of judgment, our lives take on a different form rather quickly.

There are many books on the subject, but in my humble opinion my book *Forgiveness: A Workbook for Emotional and Spiritual Freedom* will serve you completely. Other options can be as simple as writing letters of forgiveness, a ritual of burning a handwritten note that contains the names of any perpetrators or sins (mistakes you've made) or the feelings that you want to release. Be safe, please.

* Forgiveness

  Be gentle with yourself, and be patient. Practice your own forgiveness. Self-forgiveness is one way to practice good self-care. One who forgives quickly will always be healthier.
* Meditation and Silence

  There is a difference between silence and meditation, although each contains the characteristics of the other.
* Meditation

  Meditation is most often about sitting with one's eyes closed in total silence and emptying the mind, but in truth, there are many kinds. Find a teacher who works for you. YouTube is filled with thousands of guided meditations in addition to apps designed to support meditation.

  Adding meditation to your time of silence will add a richness to your experience. Meditation can be sitting in silence with your eyes closed, but there is also open-eyed meditation, walking meditation, chanting meditation, etc.
* Silence

  With silence, your eyes can be open as you embrace the opportunity to observe the world. In silence as in meditation, you will "watch" your mind and your reactions to things and then, to the best of your ability, cease forming opinions about whatever it is that you see, feel, or think!

  In silence, you listen deeply to those inner voices. In silence, you can let yourself off the hook of being "on," or from being your personality.

IN THE BEGINNING!

Begin with the provided prayer and a period of meditation. As you settle into the silence, hold this question gently in your heart: What is my intention for this time of stillness?

When you feel complete, take time to journal anything that arises. Then, sign the page as a way to commemorate this maiden voyage—and to affirm your commitment to whatever you are called to experience.

Recommended Two-Day Silent Weekend

Day 1 (assuming you begin in the evening of your first day)
Here is a prayer of surrender for you to launch your time:

There is one Life; that Life is perfect; that Life is my life now. Knowing and sensing this truth, I make myself fully available to this One as I know that this One makes Itself available to me in full measure now and always. Sensing this One surrounding me, I rest, feeling safe and confident in Its essence.

I begin this time of retreat and silence feeling safe with a willing and open mind and heart. I trust that I am guided, guarded, and protected throughout my time. I am safe. I am open and I am willing to hear and feel all that needs to be heard and felt. I am safe as I surrender into this beauty and this life. I trust this process to be loving and transformational as I release the busyness of my mind and find my own inspiration and wisdom.

With bountiful gratitude, I release this word of love to be fully demonstrated now.

And so it is!

Now, get comfortable, settle in, and begin to listen. Don't worry if you feel tired, as that is another technique of your ego—to keep you asleep. Either sleep and enjoy it or set an alarm so you don't sleep too long. Keep your journal next to you so you can record your thoughts, feelings, inspirations, and dreams.

Enjoy a cup of tea as you sit in silence with your journal and just let yourself be, let your mind wander and listen to whatever comes.

After your nighttime ritual of self-care, go to bed early, so you can feel totally rested.

What feelings have come up for you at the close of your first day? Jot some quick notes in your journal.

Try gently to not judge yourself or your experience!

Day 2 (no alarms, sleep until you feel fully rested)

Begin your day again with great self-care. Pay attention to any cravings; this new practice might invoke some uncomfortable feelings. *Feed your body, not your emotions.* Take time to write in your journal and read some spiritual material. This would be a very good time to go out for a walk if you can go somewhere where neighbors or family do not try to engage you.

Should you decide to walk, feel your feet meet the earth with each step, breathe fully, and allow yourself to observe the world closely. Think of each step as a kiss to Mother Earth. See the beauty of your surrounding world that you don't see when you are too busy.

Walk, breathe, observe!

Continue your day.

For the balance of your time, which is your choice regarding the number of days that you choose to retreat, consider a slow and easy time of layering: silence, meditation, spiritual reading (especially poetry), rest (napping is good for the soul as long you do not sleep this experience away), journaling, eating healthy food, and prayer.

Some Additional Thoughts

Throughout your time, if something catches your attention and you feel yourself begin to form an opinion, pay attention to whatever has come up and then try this statement on for size: "It's not good; it's not bad; it just is." This will help you loosen your hold on your judgments.

While judgment leaves you feeling at the mercy of opinions—your own or others'—curiosity will set you free. The statement provided will help you begin to unravel deeply held opinions and judgments. As you do, you'll find greater freedom from the inner narratives that keep you stuck.

During your time of silence, remember to speak only life-affirming **I AM** statements. Take a close and honest inventory of your self-talk. As you listen deeply, the truth of what you believe—about life and about yourself—will begin to emerge.

Even if you don't like what you hear, resist the urge to judge yourself. Instead, stay curious. Ask questions. This gentle inquiry will shift you into the mindset of the observer—where healing begins. To put it simply, be in a state of wonder.

Lastly, remain gentle upon yourself. Be kind. You are stunning in more ways than you can imagine. This practice will help you to remember this.

The following is a list of suggested activities, but please follow your heart at all times:

* Feed your body—not your emotions.
* Talk a long, refreshing bath with salts and organic fragrances.
* Walk in silence.
* Sit in silence.
* Meditate.
* Pray.
* Journal.
* Do some yoga or chair yoga.
* Rest (nap).
* Read spiritual material.
* Read spiritual poetry (poetry invokes the intuition and inspires you).
* Move slowly throughout your days.
* Take time to really breathe and get present to whatever it is that you are doing. When eating, be present to your food and slow down your eating. Nothing should feel hurried or pressured.

* After your meals, as you begin to clean up, slow down.
* As you wash the dishes, be present throughout your experience.

YOUR LAST EVENING

Before ending your time in silence, sit down one last time to take stock of your personal discovery. Record the blessings that came out of the silence of you. Write yourself a love letter and save it for a time when you need to read some words of love. Or, if you struggled, in your most authentic and transparent way, write about the struggle, be real, let yourself feel safe enough to speak the truth about what is.

Our intention creates our reality. Silence is a resource unlike anything else.

Silence has elements built within it that are powerful, although unexpected.

In the silence, you will be able to hear everything that you need to know. Trust what you hear.

RESOURCES

SUGGESTED READING LIST

- *Seven Thousand Ways to Listen: Staying Close to What Is Sacred* by Mark Nepo
- *The Surrender Experiment: My Journey into Life's Perfection* by Michael A. Singer
- *The Pathway of Roses: Paths to the Life Beautiful* by Christian D. Larson
- *Practicing the Presence: The Inspirational Guide to Regaining Meaning and a Sense of Purpose in Your Life* by Joel S. Goldsmith
- *The Life Divine* by Sri Aurobindo
- *The Voice Celestial* by Ernest S. Holmes and Fenwicke L. Holmes
- *The Dance of the Dissident Daughter: A Woman's Journey from Christian Tradition to the Sacred Feminine* by Sue Monk Kidd
- *All About Love: New Visions* by bell hooks
- *Women Who Run with the Wolves: Myths and Stories of the Wild Woman Archetype* by Clarissa Pinkola Estés

SUGGESTED MUSIC LIST

- *Liquid Silk* by Marina Raye
- Liquid Mind series by Liquid Mind
- Music created for Reiki sessions

Reminder: Look on your smartphone for meditation apps. There are a wide variety of apps and hundreds of free videos on YouTube.

WHY I CREATED THIS GUIDE

My life has been an interesting combination of pain and healing, depression and transformation. My story is rich but not unique. After years of learning to understand myself in the way that I now do, I know that it might seem to the public eye that I am an outgoing, confident woman, and I'm OK about this perception because it works for what I do. There was a time that my inner world was small, as I am an introvert through and through. While I presented as confident, I was not, but all my spiritual practices freed me up to be who I am today.

Now, I feel comfortable in my own skin. My continued growth, dedication to spiritual practices, and commitment to silence now affords me to be refreshed and renewed. I do require deep, long periods of silence and meditation to support my consistent expansion.

In my younger years, I was terrified of the quiet and of being alone, but as I have matured, the silence has become one of my greatest resources for inspiration, inner peace, and retrieving creative ideas that bring me great joy to express. A dedication to silence and meditation have helped me find ease and grace.

This life journey is not easy, but it is made easier because of my practice. My journey was not originally paved with endless possibilities. The possibilities made themselves known because of the practice of silence. Throughout my years, ideas have come to me in gentle and dramatic ways. I have found the guidance for books I've written, received full workshops to teach, and heard the inspiration to ask for help from certain others. All this support was right there within me. All I had to do was get quiet so I could actually hear what was going on.

There is a deep, infinite well of beauty and inspiration right there within you, just as there is a place within you where you have never been hurt, harmed, or injured in any way. That place can be accessed best while in the quiet of your mind. In that place, you can learn to love all of you, you can learn to forgive yourself completely and forgive those in your life who you have held as prisoner. Freedom is the reward for this work.

In this place, accessed through the silence that you will come to understand, you will find within yourself new and beautiful aspects. You'll learn to understand yourself and you will come to understand others. This will breed acceptance and compassion for humankind. And there is nothing that this world needs more of right now than bountiful love, understanding, and compassion for our entire human family.

Learn to love yourself as you are, and as you are not, and you immediately become a better human. Learn to accept responsibility for the part of the world that you have co-created and you immediately become a better human. Learn that the power and the presence of the Beloved One is who you are at the core of your being and learn to access It at any time, and you will never again feel alone or hopeless. Once again, you immediately become a better human.

What does this world need today?

More loving, kind, and compassionate humans.

MINDSHIFT: SPEAKING THE LANGUAGE OF YOUR HEART

There is a language we all intuitively knew how to speak when we were young and untainted: the language of the heart. It is the language of our birthright. A language that is powerful, creative, and deeply connected to the essence of who we are. It is a co-creative, manifesting life force. But like any powerful tool, to benefit from it, we must use it with awareness and intention.

Through the conditioning of our lives, we often forget this language—or worse, it becomes distorted by fear, shame, and external influences. Over time, we grow quiet. We disconnect from our desires. We lose sight of what truly matters. We lose our co-creative voice and deny our heart's desires.

Many of us never truly learned how to answer the question "What do I really want in my life?" with clarity and confidence. Instead, we became distracted by the noise of everyday life and stayed focused on what we don't want, what we are afraid of, and what isn't working in our lives. We got sidetracked, absorbed by responsibilities, obligations, and survival. The chaos of our humanity clouded the clarity of our soul, making it difficult to imagine what is truly possible. Metaphorically speaking, we went to sleep and became unconscious.

But something profound begins to happen when we start to remember. When we begin speaking the language of the heart again, we shift. We begin thinking in terms of possibility, worthiness, and acceptance.

We stop shrinking and apologizing for our desires. We reclaim them as sacred. When we do, life begins to take on a new texture—one woven with beauty, creativity, and abundance. We reclaim our childhood desires and dreams, and our heart opens once again. Metaphorically speaking, we begin to wake up and become conscious.

For someone new to this way of thinking, it may sound like a fairy tale—maybe even naive. That's understandable. Much of what we've been taught contradicts this approach. We've been conditioned to believe that dreaming without limits is for the foolish or the privileged—for those who don't know how hard life really is.

But that belief isn't the truth. When you were in your mother's womb, for nine months you were hardwired into the power of Life itself. And on the day of your birth, you opened your eyes and began to forget that you are one with the power of Life. We need to remember that all the genius, all the intelligence, and all the inspiration that exists is ready and waiting for you to claim it.

THE POWER WITHIN YOU

There is a creative intelligence—a life force—flowing constantly through and as you. Call it Energy, Consciousness, the universe, love, Spirit, Source . . . whatever name resonates most. It is always moving, always responding, always becoming—shaped by the molds we create through our thoughts, words, and beliefs.

Let's return to the idea of your heart's desire.

What if you could articulate the deepest longings of your soul without restriction? What if you gave yourself permission to speak with clarity and richness about what you truly want? Not what's reasonable, logical, or safe, but what's deeply true? When you do, something within you shifts. Your thoughts align. Your vibration rises. And when you begin to understand the universal truth, that your words and thoughts shape your reality, you'll realize just how powerful you've always been.

This is the time to never again speak against yourself, to stop diminishing your worth, and to stop entertaining self-doubt as if it were truth. Retrieve and redirect your attention to your power and wholeness.

HERE'S THE CHALLENGE

Most of us have been taught to disconnect from our own power. We've been taught to doubt ourselves, play it safe, and second-guess our dreams.

"Be reasonable," our caregivers said. "Stop being so self-centered. Get your head out of the clouds. Who do you think you are? What makes you think you deserve to have what you want?" And on and on it went. We internalized those messages and started to believe that we had to earn the right to dream big, or that we should just take what we're given. Yuk.

This disconnection leads to lazy thinking and lazy speaking. We say things we don't mean. We affirm limitations we don't want. And the result is a life that doesn't reflect our truth.

But Here's the Key

* We are our words.
* We are our thoughts.
* We are the creators of our experience.
* We are the result of our intention.
* We are the result of our beliefs.
* And we are the result of our attention.

Are you convinced yet?

Because the moment you take full, unwavering responsibility for your life—the moment you realize you are not a passive participant but an active co-creator—you step into alignment with the creative force that has been with you all along. Can you feel your internal power start to surge up from within?

Now what?

Let's assume you're open to this possibility. What do you do next?

Listen deeply to your heart. Not your ego. Not your fear. But the still, wise voice within you that knows what is true. Give language to your desires. Speak what you truly want. Don't justify it. Don't apologize for it. Don't explain it away. Let your language be rich and full—evocative and emotional—because it is that feeling that moves energy into form.

Speak your desires into existence. Declare them as if they are already unfolding. If you've dreamed of starting a new profession, but fear or logic have held you back—go deeper. What do you really want? Describe it. Name it. Feel it. That glass ceiling that you thought was there is self-imposed and the moment you claim the power, you can break that ceiling.

SPEAK THE LANGUAGE OF YOUR HEART

Your words are powerful. They shape the energy around you. Speak in a way that honors your life, vision, and sacred worth.

Think of a magnificent painting, rich in color and depth. Or a symphony, each note blending into the next with intention and grace. Your life is your masterpiece. You are both the artist and the canvas. The composer and the music.

So speak of your life with reverence. Speak with love, creativity, and conviction. Let your words reflect your joy, power, and limitless potential.

Your true heart is not hesitant. It is passionate, clear, intelligent, and unwavering. It does not get lost in doubt or delay. It does not waste time in self-diminishment. It simply knows. It speaks the language of acceptance, affirmation, and embodiment.

Try these affirmations on for size:

- "I am now willing to receive the good that is mine to claim."
- "I open myself to a life filled with joy, harmony, and abundance."
- "Opportunities flow to me effortlessly because I am in alignment with Life itself."
- "I claim and accept my good and my greater good from sources known and not known."

This is the language of the heart. It is a language of love, openness, and expansion. When spoken with sincerity and felt with conviction, it allows the creative force of the universe to flow freely through you.

How?

* Speak with clarity.
* Speak creatively.
* Speak responsibly.
* Speak with confidence.
* Speak with love.

Always speak in the direction of your desire and do so until your heart and mind are in sync. This is a winning combination; this is the formula for creating your heart's desires.

And then watch your life unfold in the most beautiful ways.

MINDSHIFTS FOR YOUR HEART AND SOUL

For the next thirty days, repeat this mindshift twice a day. Do it once in the morning and once before going to sleep:

> *From the power and intelligence that created me, I declare, I am now willing to be who I am. To live according to my heart's desires and my dreams. I am willing to say* no *when something is not working for me and* yes *to lovely opportunities. Feeling completely empowered, I embrace my personal power, I move forward confidently. I walk toward the horizon of my life offering me adventure and newness and amazing opportunities. I say* yes *to my life. I accept my good and my greater good daily. And I choose to continue to love myself as I am and as I am not.*
>
> *With great confidence and conviction in this word, I let it be so. And so it shall be.*

It's time for true confessions. This book—and all the work it represents—is, at its core, a self-indulgent reminder for me to be me.

I have a fond memory from many decades ago of a song sung by the beloved performer Sammy Davis Jr., a member of the iconic Rat Pack. The song was called "I've Gotta Be Me" (when you have time, look it up online!). When it was popular in the late sixties, my parents bought me the album—*I've Gotta Be Me*—so I could listen to the song over and over again.

What is your power song? You know that one that you must sing every time it comes on, the song that makes your juices flow, that makes you want to pound your fists in the air. It is that song that you will sing out loud and not care whether someone is watching. If you don't have one of those, I would identify one, because music is a dependable way to shift your mood.

I learned every word of "I've Gotta Be Me" and sang it—loudly and often—at the top of my lungs in our home. Much to my parents' chagrin, I might add, mostly because I couldn't then (and still can't) carry a tune to save my life. But oh, how I enjoyed that song! These days, only my grandchildren will tolerate me and my musical antics. Children are much better at accepting people just as they are.

The truth is, this invitation I've extended to you—this path back to your authentic self—began as an invitation to myself. This book is the result of wanting to play and engage with others in this world without pretense or apology. I want to live in a world with you—face-to-face, heart-to-heart, soul-to-soul.

I hope, as you've read these pages, you've begun to find your voice. I hope you've started honoring yourself more fully and believing in the truth of who you are: a divine being born with the birthright of brilliance. I hope you've begun to reclaim your boldness, beauty, and brilliance. This life is far too short to play small.

A better you is a gift to the planet. That's not just a feel-good affirmation—it's something I believe with my whole heart. Of course, some might dismiss that as idealistic or overly ambitious. But let's look a little closer.

I'm not encouraging you to turn your journey of authenticity into some kind of attention-grabbing performance, like the endless stream of flash-in-the-pan influencers on social media chasing millions of likes and followers. That's not what this is about.

This stunning planet we live on—and everything it contains—is a living, breathing, pulsing creation of energy and life, of which we are each an integral part. We share the air. We share the resources. We are connected—energetically, intuitively, emotionally. The only difference is in how deeply we experience that connection.

Some people experience it profoundly, with clarity and certainty. Others sense it faintly, without fully knowing what they're feeling. But the connection itself? It's never in question—only our awareness of it is. And the more aware we are, the more powerfully we can participate in shaping the world around us.

You might have heard the saying that a butterfly flapping its wings in Brazil can set off a tornado in Texas. Whether or not that's scientifically accurate (and it probably isn't), the metaphor holds weight. Small actions do matter. Tiny shifts in thought, subtle acts of courage, quiet whispers of love—they ripple outward in ways we may never see.

This is what I call the authenticity effect: Your most delicate motion, rooted in truth, can set powerful forces into motion. Your choice to speak up, heal, rise, and love louder—it could be the beginning of something vast and beautiful.

Have you ever truly considered just how much you are a part of that potentiality?

Consider this: A healed, whole, integrated version of you will have an entirely different experience of life than a fearful, self-denying version of you. You will make different decisions. You will radiate different energy. You will create different outcomes—not only for yourself, but for everyone around you.

Oh, the beauty of being a teacher, speaker, coach, and author is just how much I have grown due to whatever it is that I am offering in each particular moment. Even now, in April 2025, only days after my birthday, I experienced a major shift.

All my life I have made the major error of always believing that I was at the cause for someone's unhappiness or discomfort. I had the absolute worst habit of thinking that it was about me, that I wasn't enough and so I deserved to be ignored, unappreciated, and virtually unseen. It never felt good, but I was never surprised because I just wasn't worth it.

But the work is working, and it is the whole point of this book. I received some news about someone who, years before, had stopped talking to me for reasons I will probably never thoroughly know or understand.

Instead of responding from my old feelings being sparked, I reacted totally differently, with acceptance and forgiveness.

Here is the gift of the work and of the transformation. I was left feeling free of any wanting, free of needing, and free to simply realize that what I actually want is to live a life standing next to other strong, self-realized, independent people. This is how I want to finish my life—strong and expressed among my tribe.

It was sobering and wonderful to take an inventory of myself, and as I basked in the rewards of this, other wonderful news arrived. That is, of course, a result of one of the classic spiritual metaphysical truths: My high vibe attracted other high-vibe situations.

Living a life of authenticity is to live a life of freedom. This was my promise to you at the beginning of this book. When you find peace with who you are, you will allow yourself to live a life of joy, to accept people and life as they are without constantly needing things to be different. An authentic life will deliver to you right on your doorstep opportunities to express and excel at whatever you want.

Please affirm yourself with me right now:

> *I am one with the intelligence, inspiration, and love that has created all that I see, know, feel, and am. I surrender to this Creative Source and allow myself to be loved and supported by It at every turn. All that I am is because of this intelligence and love, as It leaves me knowing that I am Love Itself.*
>
> *With every step I take forward in this consciousness of love that created my life, I do so with my head held high, while walking completely grounded in the truth of my being. I live a life in which I get to express my talents, investigate my interests, and expand my world. I am completely plugged in to this source and power and so I feel safe. Safe to be who I am, how I am, without exception.*
>
> *With this way of being, I am incredibly happy with and appreciative for the journey that got me here. And I trust that my life will continue to unfold right before my eyes in the most glorious ways possible. I accept all*

my potentiality. I accept the bounty of my success. I accept my life as vibrant health. I accept all the love that shows up, and I accept the continued adventure that is in store for me.

Life is good, and this day is the most glorious day of my life. I claim this as so with the deepest sense of gratitude and I allow it to be my reality right here and right now.

And so it is!

ACKNOWLEDGMENTS

Thank you to my husband, who always says yes to my wild and wonderful ideas; to Joel Fotinos, who opened the door to a new part of myself; to my coach and friend, Julia Matias, who continually calls me into the "more of me"; and once again, to my Spiritual Teacher, Rita Sperling—without whom I would be only a shell of who I have become.

ABOUT THE AUTHOR

Lee Seidenberg

Michelle Wadleigh is a spiritual firestarter, a master teacher of metaphysics, and the founder of **Planned Happiness Institute**. Known for her blend of fierce love, radical truth-telling, and deep spiritual wisdom, she has spent more than two decades igniting transformation on stages, classrooms, coaching rooms, and spiritual communities.

As the **Founding Spiritual Director of The Center for Spiritual Living North Jersey**, Michelle built a thriving community rooted in authenticity, healing, and spiritual freedom. She later served at the **highest levels of leadership within Centers for Spiritual Living**, helping shape the direction of the global movement. She holds a **Doctorate of Divinity**, is a certified Empowerment coach, and is widely regarded as a teacher who strips away every bit of spiritual fluff and invites you into real, soul-level transformation.

Michelle is the **author of many transformational books**, including *Shadow Work: A Spiritual Path to Healing and Integration*; *Forgiveness: A Workbook for Emotional and Spiritual Freedom*; *40 Days to Freedom; Prosperous Me*; and *Dance Like Nobody's Watching*. Her 2025 book, *Shadow Work: A Spiritual Path to Healing and Integration*, received both **Gold and Bronze COVR Awards,** a **Living Now Book Award Bronze Medal**, and an **Arts Award from Centers for Spiritual Living.** Earlier in her ministry, she was honored with the **Shirley Chisholm Award for Excellence in Women in Ministry**.

Born and raised in New Jersey, Michelle brings a soulful, slightly rebellious flavor to her work—equal parts mystical badass, tender guide, and truth-teller who refuses to let anyone shrink on her watch. She is passionate about helping people reclaim their power, forgive what holds them back, and step into a life of sacred audacity, grace, and unapologetic joy.

Michelle lives with her husband Neil Pinkman in Denville, New Jersey, and is the proud mother of three sons and the delighted grandmother of four magical beings, all of whom keep her grounded, inspired, and fiercely committed to the healing of future generations. Whether teaching, writing, or lovingly disrupting someone's limitations, she remains devoted to one mission: **to wake people up to the brilliance, freedom, and divine power already alive within them**.